Richmond
1887
A Quaker Drama
Unfolds

Mark Minear

Friends United Press
Richmond, Indiana

Library of Congress Cataloging-in-Publication Data

Minear, Mark, 1953–
    Richmond, 1887.

        Bibliography: p.
        1. Richmond Friends Conference (1887 : Richmond, Ind.)
2. Society of Friends—Indiana—History—19th century.
3. Indiana—Church history.   I. Title.
BX7648.V8M56 1987   289.6'3   87-7603
ISBN 0-913408-98-0

To my family—
Karla, Emily, and Andrew,

and to the family of Friends!

Contents

Comments and Acknowledgments

The Richmond Conference of 1887 was both an ending and a beginning. This gathering was a major event for "Orthodox-Gurneyite" Quakers as it culminated the spiritual liveliness of the preceding twenty-seven years beginning with the Indiana Yearly Meeting sessions of 1860. The conference was also the first step toward the establishment of a new Quaker institution, the Five Years Meeting officially founded in 1902 and known today as Friends United Meeting. The implications of the discussions and decisions of this conference are still being realized today!

It is important to note that many of the "Orthodox-Gurneyite" Friends of a century ago considered themselves to be the only true Friends in America. After the separations, some of these "Gurneyite" Quakers wrote as if the other Friends from the "Hicksite" and "Wilburite" traditions weren't really Friends any longer. (Of course, some Friends from those traditions also wrote from the perspective that they were the only true Friends as well.) It is hoped that the readers would realize this attitude. I do not hold such an opinion and would want the entire family of Friends to benefit from the historical research.

The cast of characters in Part II does not exhaust the list of significant leaders among Friends one hundred years ago. Several other character sketches could have been written. However, the in-depth look at the nine personalities does give a flavor of the quality of life among

Friends of that generation.

This book was certainly not accomplished on my own. The grace of God, the support of my family, and the encouragement of many friends have brought this work thus far. I also owe a debt of gratitude to Friends of several meetings (especially First Friends Church of Des Moines with whom I currently worship), to the community of faculty and students at the Earlham School of Religion while I did research on my master's thesis, to the library departments of three Quaker colleges (Earlham, Haverford, and William Penn), to the staffs of Friends United Meeting and Friends United Press, and to the many Friends who share a vision of God's love for the future of the Religious Society of Friends. Thank you!

Mark Minear
January 1987

Prologue

Quakerism Prior to 1860: Separations

Since the Richmond Conference of 1887 was a gathering of only "Orthodox-Gurneyite" Yearly Meetings, it might be well to begin with a look at the Great Separation of 1827-28 within the Religious Society of Friends in America. The events leading up to the separation of the "Hicksite" and "Orthodox" Friends are very complicated and can lead one to much confusion and many theories. The causes can best be understood when seen coming out of the context of the period of Quaker Quietism.

Howard Brinton gives an understanding of this condition of being inwardly detached from the world:

> The Quakers from about 1700 to 1850, particularly those of the eighteenth century, have been frequently spoken of as quietists. Quietism is the doctrine that every self-centered trait or activity must be suppressed or quieted in order that the divine may find unopposed entrance to the soul. . . For the quietist, the search for God begins in removing obstructions, such as self-will and worldly desires, greed, pride, and lust, so that the inner room may be ready for the divine quest if he should enter.[1]

Robert Barclay in his *Apology* encourages the believer to quiet the creaturely activity by stilling the body and halting the roving of the imagination. This worship on the basis of silence put one experientially in touch with the Spirit of God.

As Quietism was combined with the habits, customs, and forms of Friends, becoming more fixed in the later generations of the 1700s, Bible reading, theological reasoning, and religious education were not given a place of priority. Friends were not immune, however, to religious, political and intellectual developments in the larger society.

Historian Elbert Russell cites four basic causes of the separation. These were outside forces which placed insurmountable pressure on the Society, then based largely on Quietism.

1. Around the time of the Revolutionary War there was a new spirit of democracy and personal freedom which asserted the natural rights of all people politically, socially and religiously. Even though Friends were quite isolated, they directly faced this pressure as a revolt occurred against the discipline and the authority of the elders.

2. This tendency was encouraged by a second movement, the rise of rationalism known as the Enlightenment. Voltaire in France and Thomas Paine in America gave impetus to this movement which influenced Hannah Barnard of New York, Micah Ruggles and the New Light movement of New England, and Elias Hicks, who sought to rationalize his own theology.

3. Changes were occurring socially as well. There were growing differences between country and city Friends. Wealth, education, communications, culture--all became separating factors within the Society.

4. Many Friends, mainly those of the large cities, experienced ecumenicity with the Evangelical Movement of the Second Great Awakening in the early 1800s. Evangelical Quakers, such as David Sands and Stephen Grellet, sought to re-emphasize Orthodox beliefs by simply adding them to the Quietistic Mysticism. Job Scott and Elias Hicks made the Inner Light theology of Quietism all-sufficient. Many Evangelical Friends from London Yearly Meeting were influenced by the Church of England. Several visited America in the early 1800s and applied the pressure of guidance from the "mother" church. Isaac and Anna Braithwaite (Joseph Bevan Braithwaite's parents),

William Forster, George and Anna Jones, and,
particularly, Thomas Shillitoe were a few of those
outspoken in the Orthodox views.[2]

The Great Separation itself could be understood through the representation of four men. All were steeped in the Quietistic tradition, but each represented a particular fourth, or single aspect, of the total message of Friends. Samuel Bettle, clerk of Philadelphia Yearly Meeting in 1827, maintained his authority as an elder and defended the Orthodox view. John Comly, the assistant clerk, was greatly concerned by the intolerance of those who considered themselves Orthodox. Thomas, Shillitoe, the shoemaker and preacher from London, was a champion of the Orthodox views as he held the historical work of Jesus as essential. Elias Hicks, the farmer and preacher from Long Island, held that Jesus was merely a great example of one who lived by the guidance of the Divine Inward Principle.

The two sides drew their lines, and Philadelphia began a separation that several other yearly meetings would experience. Those who sided with Hicks and who received the name Hicksites were not always necessarily enthusiastic followers of Hicks' ideas, but they stood with Hicks for freedom of thought on all religious matters. Rufus Jones gives his interpretation of the event in *The Later Periods of Quakerism*:

> Here was the place where a loving spirit, tender appreciation and methods of reconciliation would have worked wonders if only those Elders had known how to employ such forces. This was the critical moment and here was the watershed that shaped the course of the coming movements. The inability to maintain "unity," which meant to these Elders uniformity of doctrine pushed them over into positive opposition to the man whose immense vogue and influence disturbed them. The immmediate effect of this action of the Elders was the aligning of the two parties in a much more definite way than before. Most Friends were from now on loyal sympathizers of Hicks or supporters of the opposing Elders.[3]

The split in Philadelphia left two-thirds as Hicksite and one-third as Orthodox. The same percentage occurred in New York Yearly Meeting the next spring. Baltimore and Ohio went three-fourths and one-half Hicksite, respectively. Indiana remained almost entirely Orthodox. Separations did not occur in New England, Virginia, North Carolina,

London, and Dublin. The numbers of Hicksite and Orthodox Friends in America were equal. But with Dublin and London, the Orthodox was the larger group. Russell comments:

> On the whole, the Orthodox were the more promising group. The great majority of the official class--elders, overseers, ministers and members of the meeting for sufferings were found in this branch. The city Friends, especially in Philadelphia, New York, and Baltimore, constituted the more influential element among them and contributed a greater degree of education, culture, and wealth. They were a positive and unified group. All who were undecided between the two contending parties or who refused to take sides or who were not decidedly Orthodox in doctrine were rapidly disowned by the Orthodox. No one was allowed to "sit on the fence"---all who were not for them were against them. They were thus a fairly homogeneous, disciplined body, united by positive doctrinal beliefs, which carried with them by implication a working program and for the moment, at least, opened the way for progress.[4]

Rufus Jones gives the example of Radnor Monthly Meeting in Pennsylvania, where between 1825 and 1830 one hundred and eighty-two members were disowned because they joined the Hicksites. Almost that number again were disowned in the next twenty years for a variety of reasons. This indicates the condition of decline that the Society in general faced.

Immediately after the separation, most Orthodox bodies raced to issue declarations of their position. These declarations gave forth the fundamental elements of Christian doctrine and also justified the actions of separating. By the end of 1828 Indiana, North Carolina, Ohio, Philadelphia, and New York had all published Orthodox statements of faith. Many used extracts from early statements of London Yearly Meeting.

Despite the numerous declarations by individual yearly meetings, it was not enough for the Orthodox. In August of 1829, representatives of the Orthodox yearly meetings met in Philadelphia for a conference to prepare an inclusive declaration of faith called *The Testimony of the Society of Friends on the Continent of America.*

> This document is more in the nature of a real formulation of faith than the preceding ones, since it not only expresses

the adherence of Friends to the accepted Orthodox Christian principles, but also delineates Friends special testimonies.

This formulation stands out as the one great corporate declaration before the "Richmond Declaration of Faith" over fifty years later. It was the product and climax of the whole Orthodox movement from its beginning in the later part of the 18th century, as in a somewhat similar way the "Richmond Declaration" was the culmination of the evangelical movement of the middle 19th century. Within a short time after its publication it was approved and accepted by the Yearly Meetings of Ohio, Baltimore, North Carolina, Philadelphia, New York, Virginia, and New England.[5]

The Hicksites in New York also issued a statement of doctrine which was quite Orthodox as well, primarily due to a law suit over property. But in the end, freedom in doctrinal expression became the established policy. Doctrines were not held as essentials of the Christian faith, but instead as fruits of it.[6]

Clearly, the Orthodox and Hicksite Friends rapidly went their own ways. The Orthodox sought purity in doctrine, the Hicksites tolerance. The Orthodox emphasized the historical manifestation of Christ; the Hicksites continued with the mystical manifestation of Christ. They promptly divided up the Quaker heritage, developed their own religious vocabulary, and found ecumenicity with a different set of denominations.

Although London Yearly Meeting sided with the Orthodox, the diversity of Friends was present in the yearly meeting and they remained together. They worshipped together and transacted business together, because tolerance was a high ideal. However, English Friends did experience some tension due to Isaac Crewdson and the Beaconite Controversy in 1835.

Crewdson combined his extreme Evangelical view of the scriptures with a paranoia of "Hicksism". He sought to correct Friends on the doctrine of the Inner Light. Crewdson found support from the Braithwaite family in England and Elisha Bates of Ohio.

Two weighty Friends over the next few years were to be greatly influenced by the Beaconite Controversy. Joseph Bevan Braithwaite was a young Quaker who made the decision to remain with Friends in 1840, even though several members of his family left with Crewdson.

The second Friend to be greatly influenced by Crewdson's book, *A Beacon to the Society of Friends*, was Joseph John Gurney. Gurney gave the Orthodox Friends a solid place to stand with his Biblical scholarship, systematic theology, and emphasis upon education. Gurney served on the London Yearly Meeting committee which was appointed to investigate the problem that Crewdson had started in Lancashire Quarterly Meeting and to restore unity there. About three hundred Friends eventually seceded with Crewdson, calling themselves Evangelical Friends. Many of this number later joined the Plymouth Brethren. In the end, Gurney found himself between the extremes of the Hicksites and the Beaconites. He recorded in his diary:

> First, on the danger of conversation on the supposed unsoundness of others; on varying opinions; on American and supposed English Hicksism. Secondly, on the vast importance of our proclamation of orthodox doctrine, not to trench on the "anointing" or on those things which we have found experimentally to be truly precious. Earnestly do I desire that the evil, so much dreaded, and which I believe to be nonexistent, may not be fretted into being.[7]

Gurney traveled to America with hopes to restore unity and win back the Hicksites. Yet, he had no communication with them and even was opposed by many of the Orthodox body, particularly older members. Gurney did have influence with American young Friends as they became enthusiastic about the scriptures and education. But opposition came forth in John Wilbur, a New England Friend who wanted to conserve Quaker practice of the Quietistic type.

Wilbur regarded Gurney as encouraging dangerous tendencies in Bible readings and lectures, Bible Schools, and Bible Societies. These activities promoted advanced preparation and organization. Although they were quite close in theology, Gurney and Wilbur differed greatly in practice. Because of this, Gurney received opposition in New England, Philadelphia and Ohio.

New England experienced a separation in 1845 with five hundred members remaining with Wilbur. The 6,500 members of the "Larger Body" won the court battle over the possession of property.

In 1849 New York Yearly Meeting summoned a conference of Orthodox Friends in America to meet in Baltimore "to consider the present tried state of the Society, and to labor for its restoration to unity and fellowship."[8] Although they were invited, Philadelphia and Ohio did not send representatives on the grounds that only the "Larger Body" from New England was invited. The conference met again in 1851 and 1853 to encourage Philadelphia and Ohio to attend and recognize the Larger Body. Ohio responded with their own Wilburite-Gurneyite separation in 1854 due to a debate to decide which body in New England to recognize. This was disastrous to a yearly meeting which previously cut off communication with the Hicksites in 1828.

Numerous separations of the Wilbur-Gurney concern over matters of practice continued throughout the century at monthly, quarterly, and yearly meeting levels.

The split in Ohio threatened to divide Philadelphia. In short, Philadelphia Friends preserved their yearly meeting by suspending all correspondence for that year. This became the established policy, and Philadelphia isolated itself from all other yearly meetings. Philadelphia was able to hold both factions--Gurneyite and Wilburite--together.

The majority of the membership of this yearly meeting was very pronounced and emphatic in its conservative attitude. But J.J. Gurney had left a definite influence with a strong minority. They sought to be forward-looking and believed that the Gurney movement provided the brightest future. This group provided the founding and leadership of Haverford College. They also were the creators, editors, and publishers of a new literary journal, the *Friends' Review*.

While the *Friends' Review* was initiated out of the days of the Gurney-Wilbur tension by the Gurneyites in 1847, the Wilburites in Philadelphia continued with *The Friend*, which had become the organ for Orthodox Quietism. It was started in 1827, at the time of the previous separation.

The *Friends' Review* became a strong vehicle of Gurneyite concerns to Friends as they traveled westward along the frontier. Friends meetings established schools and First-day schools and found that the change of life and distance from the stable yearly meetings of the East provided greater freedom for their religious expressions. The Bible was once again studied in the home. This was accompanied by expressions of vocal prayer. All this cultural and societal change modified Quakerism on the frontier, not to mention the receptiveness to and influence of other Christian denominations.

Gurneyite Friends found themselves open to the ecumenical Church. In 1857 and 1858 the *Friends' Review* started to publish various accounts of interdenominational revivals in some of the eastern cities. These revivals were being led by laymen. They were informal and lacked the emotionalism of earlier revivals. To the more flexible, Gurneyite Quakers, these services were found to be appealing. Wanting to encourage such renewal, the *Review* suggested that some Friends might wish to hold such informal gatherings in their homes. These "reading circles" or "social-religious meetings" would include reading from the Bible or other devotional literature, discussion, testimonies, and prayer. One of the first of these reading circles was started in Richmond in the home of Charles F. Coffin in December of 1858.[9]

This circle provided the freedom for a little group to meet on an evening at the beginning of the 1860 Indiana Yearly Meeting sessions to plan a special meeting for the younger Friends.

Many other grass roots Bible classes, prayer meetings, and discussion groups were springing up all through the Society. Allen Jay's Bible class at Greenfield, Indiana, which met on First-day afternoon, was another example of new interest and new life coming from the young people.

A revival, indeed, had begun. Perhaps it doesn't do justice to the movement to place its beginning at a certain time, a certain place, or with a certain people. But what was significant was that it had started. And the course for the Orthodox Friends, particularly the Gurneyite faction, would be full of adventure, change, blessing, and controversy. Allen Jay himself thought that the revival started out in the little community of Greenfield. But he writes:

> Other localities have claimed that the movement was born
> in their midst and that some special person was the
> instrument in bringing it about. It may have been that the
> sign of the "going in the tops of the mulberry trees" may
> have been first heard by those who never said much about
> it. The Master will know where to bestow the crown.[10]

Indiana Yearly Meeting of 1860 and Revivalism

The year was 1860. The day was October 7. The place was Richmond, Indiana. The event was the annual gathering of the Indiana Yearly Meeting of the Religious Society of Friends. "The hour was long prepared for, the time was ripe, and suddenly the fire was kindled, no matter who struck off the first spark."[1]

From these yearly meeting sessions, one may look to the preceding years as well as to the following years of Orthodox Quakerism with greater understanding and appreciation. These annual sessions in Richmond, Indiana, marked the end of a search and the beginning of a new era among Quakers, especially younger Friends. They would become the leaders of a new generation of Quaker thought, practice, and expansion.

At the beginning of the 1860 annual sessions, there was a small gathering in the home of Charles and Rhoda Coffin. Charles was the clerk of Indiana Yearly Meeting, succeeding his father Elijah, who had been clerk for many years. Charles and Rhoda were present. Charles' parents were there. Also meeting with this family in the library were John Henry Douglas, Harriet Steer, Murray Shipley, and Dr. David Judkins. Here was a group of people, particularly younger Friends, who were longing for a deeper, more refreshing, more fulfilling Christian experience. As Rhoda penned it herself:

> The younger people had no means of showing their love to God by any active service. They were required to use certain modes of dress and language, abstain from all relaxations and amusements, music and singing were prohibited. Even singing a hymn at home was very doubtful, not to be encouraged, an evidence of "creaturely activity" of which there was great fear. It was a narrow path, a "guarded education," but the guards were so strong and high that the breathing of the pure air of contact with other Christians was almost shut off. The pure flow of Christ-like thought was obstructed by repression. . . . There were many hungering and thirsting for the water of life, but few to give it. It was, however, soon to flow freely.

> At the beginning of the Yearly Meeting of 1860 a company met at our house to consult as to what should be done, or rather *could* be done. . . after a season of prayer and consultion we decided to send a written request to the Yearly Meeting for the privilege of holding an evening meeting for sacred worship in the "Old" Whitewater Meeting House for those in the younger walks of life.[2]

During those yearly meeting sessions some weighty ministers from other yearly meetings were also in attendance. Among them were Sybil Jones of New England, Lindley M. Hoag of Iowa, and Rebecca T. Updegraff of Ohio.

Rebecca Updegraff was the mother of David B. Updegraff. She and her husband were close friends of the well-known revivalist Charles G. Finney, who was very influential upon their Christian lives. Rebecca believed very strongly in the necessity of a conversion experience.

Sybil Jones, a minister and co-laborer alongside of her husband Eli, had a powerful and moving ministry. They traveled with missionary zeal to Great Britain, Ireland, Norway, Germany, Switzerland, France, Liberia, and Sierra Leone. Sybil had experienced a very powerful call to ministry in 1850. This is her recorded story:

> The evidence had been very clear, but the feelings of unfitness for the work seemed to hedge up the way entirely, and I thought unless some person would come to me and tell me the Lord required it and would fit me for the work, I would not take a step. I thought I could not receive it but from some one clothed with gospel authority; and in looking over this class I selected dear Benjamin Seebohm, who I knew was somewhere in America. . . . Our monthly

> meeting day arrived, and, though my health was so frail
> that I had gotten out to meeting but little for some time, I
> felt an almost irresistible impression to go. I accordingly
> went. As I entered the door almost the first person I met
> was Benjamin Seebohm. I could not have been surprised at
> the appearance of any person. . . . The meeting gathered
> under a solemnity. . . . and after a time of very solemn
> silence, dear Benjamin arose and took up an individual case,
> and so exactly described my feelings and the service that no
> doubt remained but the Most High had sent him with this
> message to me.[3]

Benjamin Seebohm was converted to Christ and convinced of Quakerism by Stephen Grellet, the well-known Quaker evangelist and missionary of the early nineteenth century. Stephen Grellet helped Quakers in the early 1800s to experience an evangelical faith and to build a solid Orthodox foundation. Now Grellet's disciple, Benjamin Seebohm, is used of God to challenge Sybil Jones into the ministry. Her ministry at Indiana Yearly Meeting in 1860 set off another explosion of Quaker evangelism. It is intriguing that Grellet had an indirect, and yet almost direct, influence upon the Quaker Revival Movement, because, as Rufus Jones put it: "Sybil Jones was to be a chosen instrument in inaugurating the awakening itself."[4]

Elbert Russell noted that it was the two visiting ministers, Lindley M. Hoag and Rebecca T. Updegraff, who requested the appointment of an evening meeting for the youth during the 1860 Indiana Yearly Meeting gathering. Their request was seconded by Sybil Jones and some other Friends, many of whom were from Murray Shipley's home meeting in Cincinnati Meeting. Murray Shipley had been a part of that small group which had gathered at the Coffin home. The proposal did meet with a great deal of opposition, but it was finally granted. It was understood that the older attenders were to keep silent, not to preach or be heard on this occasion, and that the "babes and sucklings should have a chance to break forth."[5]

First-day evening, October 7, 1860, became a spiritually pivotal date on many, many calendars. Exactly how many attended this appointed meeting is uncertain. Rhoda Coffin recorded that it was estimated there were one thousand persons in attendance. Rufus Jones wrote that there were more than one thousand. Luke Woodard recorded that the seating capacity, including the galleries, was 1,500 or more, and it was densely filled. Elijah Coffin recorded in his journal that there were "not less than two thousand present, a memorable time."[6] And another first hand participant wrote that the seating capacity was estimated between two and three thousand, and it was completely filled. This anonymous attender recorded quite an interesting account of that evening's meeting:

> The ministers spoke very briefly and impressively. A solemn hush pervaded the vast assemblage. Many afterwards stated that they could feel the Divine presence. Presently a young person gave an expression to his aspirations for a life of greater devotion to the cause of Christ. In rapid succession he was followed by others from every part of the huge building. Not only were there heard testimonies, aspirations, exhortations, confessions, but there were numerous prayers for guidance to a higher life, for forgiveness of past sins, for an outpouring of the Spirit. In those days, when some one knelt in prayer, the entire congregation rose, took off their hats and turned about so as to face the rear of the house. I still remember the reverberation caused by the rising and turning of this large audience. When the prayer, usually quite brief at this meeting, came to an end, there were the same noise and confusion when seats were resumed. After many prayers had been uttered, one of the ministers in the gallery suggested that for the remainder of this meeting, in order to save time, Friends should keep their seats during the time of prayer. And so for the remainder of the meeting the clatter of the shuffling of five or six thousand feet was unheard. The meeting began at seven in the evening and continued till after midnight. During those five hours several hundred testimonies, prayers, confessions, yearnings, votive offerings were heard. There were still burdened hearts but the ministers with reluctance thought the time had come for the close of this memorable meeting. Thus was launched that great movement whose results at that time could not be foretold.[7]

Rhoda Coffin wrote as a planner of the meeting, as an attender, and as one who was deeply moved by the gathering:

> The solemnity of the Meeting could only be *felt*—it could not be written; there was no form, no leader. The young people were told the purpose of the Meeting and that it was theirs. Murray Shipley, Dr. David Judkins, Charles and myself spoke for the first time publicly, avowing our allegiance to Christ. When we were arranging for the Meeting, I knew that it would be my privilege to own my

> Lord, and publicly to enlist in His service. When I declared
> that I was His, and He was my Saviour; and repeated the
> text, "Let others do as they may, I will serve the Lord," I
> was loosed and set free, and I came out of that Meeting
> with a heart full of love to God, and a spirit to *do* His will.
>
> Hundreds gave their testimony for Christ or offered their
> first public prayer. There was no confusion, no haste, no
> urging or calling on anyone to speak. The Lord was
> working with great power, and when the Meeting closed,
> we were all astonished when told that it was 1.30 o'clock in
> the morning.[8]

The *Friends' Review* said, editorially, that this evening meeting was
"a season of remarkable awakening and divine favour."[9]

After the close of yearly meeting, Sybil Jones had a concern to meet
with those who had taken part in this special evening service. About
150 met with her at the home of Charles and Rhoda Coffin. "Our
drawing room, library, and hall were filled. It was a most interesting
meeting. We invited them all to come again on each Sabbath evening,
and for more than four years our home was opened every week and large
numbers attended."[10]

A correspondent from Indiana Yearly Meeting to the *Friends' Review*
penned these words in regard to the 1860 Indiana Yearly Meeting
sessions. There is no doubt that the evening service for the younger
Friends on First-day had much to do with the flavor of the entire yearly
meeting.

> Our Yearly Meeting this year has been unusually large, and
> it is the general opinion that we never before had such
> evidences of the prevalence of real, vital religion amongst
> us. It has been spoken of as a genuine revival. Great
> harmony has prevailed; indeed, the character of the meeting
> throughout has been such, that things have ascended that
> we lived to see this day.[11]

Perhaps the words of John Henry Douglas written reflectively in a
letter to a friend more than fifty years later best reveals the importance
of this beginning.

> In the providence of God a very strong encouragement was
> given to the revival spirit and work by that never to be
> forgotten Sabbath night evening during [Indiana] Yearly

> Meeting in 1860. . . . It is well written up in Rhoda M.
> Coffin's journal. This meeting was attended and approved
> by many leading Friends among them Lindley M. Hoag,
> Sybil Jones, Rebecca Updegraff and others. It had been on
> my heart for years and I could not rest until it was granted.
> Then the revival wave rose higher and higher in many parts
> of America.[12]

From a small group in a home to more than one thousand in a meetinghouse and then back again to that same house for a crowded afterglow service of 150 people—one single week marked a new era for Orthodox Friends.

QUAKERISM AFTER 1860 AND THE CIVIL WAR

From the 1840s to the 1870s, the Orthodox Friends in the United States continued to become a more diversified body. Not only were the differences between Wilburites and Gurneyites becoming increasingly clear, but the Gurneyites continued to experience diversity among themselves. The basic differences between the Wilburite "conservatives" and the Gurneyite "liberals" were not theological or doctrinal in nature. The differences were in regard to the "practice" of the faith.

Gurneyite Friends were becoming intentional about their faith. They were beginning to systematically build the Church. Education was greatly valued by the Gurneyites. They became deliberate about the study and reading of the Bible. They became theological through Bible meetings and discussions. They became evangelical as they expressed their witness through Bible tracts and other literature. They became ecumenical as the advanced culture was bringing people together and because they were opening themselves to other Christians. They became progressive as the movement west on the frontier presented them with new challenges and new opportunities.

Some of the Gurneyite adherants were not able to withstand all this change, and, thus, the change made it difficult for the Gurneyites to hold together in unity. One must recognize that Orthodox Friends had been through two major separations in two generations. This partial hold of the original Quaker understanding of the Gospel was then combined with the freedom to be intentional, theological, evangelical, ecumenical, and progressive. Some Gurneyite Quakers held their ground in the stability of the East Coast culture of Baltimore, New York, and Philadelphia, while others marched toward Wilmington, Richmond, Oskaloosa, Wichita, Newberg, and Whittier and the changing culture of the frontier. In addition to all of this, a new generation of young Friends began to step forward in leadership with the Indiana Yearly Meeting awakening of 1860.

The Civil War would put a hold on the changing events for Friends. All Quakers thoughout the nation would be touched somehow through this War Between the States. The Gurneyite Friends were deeply concerned about the issues of justice and peace. Therefore, the war would redirect their emphases for a while from theological issues to social issues. The Quaker testimonies of equality and peace would both be challenged as well as be placed in a tension with each other.

Most of the anti-slavery tension within Friends was manifest prior to the war. Most notable is the separation in Indiana in 1843. All Friends would have been considered anti-slavery. However, some Friends were radical abolitionists. Levi Coffin, the "President of the Underground Railroad," and Charles Osborn, a recorded minister and first editor of *The Antislavery Standard*, were leaders of this radical group based in Newport, Indiana. Other Friends of the yearly meeting were uncomfortable with the abolitionist practices which were considered illegal by the government. They were also concerned with the mixing with other denominations and the "hireling ministry" that the other anti-slavery groups had.

After the Indiana Yearly Meeting sessions of 1842, many of the radicals thought it best to hold a conference, which they did in February of 1843. Twelve monthly meetings, which made up five quarterly meetings, formed a separate yearly meeting known as the Indiana Yearly Meeting of Anti-Slavery Friends. In the next few years the yearly meeting slowly reunited.

As it became more evident that war was inevitable, Friends would begin to consider their equality testimony in the face of their peace testimony. Some of the young men in the Society joined with the Union Army and participated in the war. Others refused the draft and even the payment of the $300.00 fine. Many suffered abuse, especially in the South where they were held in suspicion due to their anti-slavery sentiment. During the 1800s prior to the war, many Friends had moved into the North to stay clear of the South's position on slavery.

Much of the leadership of Friends worked hard during the Civil War years to seek exemption for Friends from military duty. Other Friends were quite active in ministering to freed slaves coming North during and immediately after the war. They sought to provide food, clothing, shelter, work, education, etc.—anything to help these slaves work from owning nothing to self-sufficiency.

All of these concerns surrounding the war provided Friends with an opportunity for service but also a distraction from intentionally building the Church of the future. However, the revival, initiated in 1860, would only be postponed and not cancelled.

THE REVIVAL CONTINUES

Alex H. Hay in his thesis, "The Pastoral System Among Friends," suggests that the development of higher education among Quakers was an important factor in preparing for the revival. He points out that eighteen educational institutions were started between 1830 and 1870, including five colleges and nine high schools. This Gurneyite influence upon the young Friends paved the way for the renewal to re-ignite after the war. During 1865-1870, Earlham College, Center Grove Academy near Oskaloosa, Iowa, and Whittier College, then at Salem, Iowa, all revealed a great interest in religious thought and renewal.

The "social-religious" gatherings continued to spread across the Midwest, and one by one these meetings were transferred to the meetinghouses. Two controversial revival services occurred during the year 1867. One was led by two traveling ministers among Bear Creek Friends in Iowa, and the other one was held at the meetinghouse of Walnut Ridge Friends in Indiana.

The radical Walnut Ridge Revival is the more well-known of the two. A small group of Friends, after meeting in a home for their "tract-reading meeting," decided to gather at the meetinghouse and pray for a community awakening. After gathering informally for several Sunday evenings, individuals would come under conviction of sin and go to the front pew, the "mourner's bench," where the leaders would pray for them. Many seekers began to come, and the meetings grew in number. Even elders and overseers joined those meetings of great evangelical and emotional fervor. But many of the more conservative and older Friends were frightened and disappointed with this new movement.

Such was also the case at Bear Creek in Iowa. Stacy Bevan and John S. Bond were Friends traveling with minutes, one from Honey Creek Monthly Meeting and the other from Bangor Monthly Meeting, both of Iowa. While they were journeying to visit Friends in Kansas, they stopped at Bear Creek for a meeting for worship. Stacy Bevan's account of this meeting is worth reading in full, because it is indicative of what would happen across the Midwest.

We made a brief stay at Bear Creek and held one public meeting at least, where the power of the Lord was wonderfully manifested. Many hearts were reached and all broken up, which was followed by sighs and sobs and prayers, confessions and great joy for sins pardoned and burdens rolled off, and precious fellowship of the redeemed. But alas, some of the dear old Friends mistook this outbreak of the power of God for excitement and wild fire, and tried to close the meeting, but we kept cool and held the strings, and closed the meeting orderly. But after meeting they administered a large dose of "elder tea," with a request to make tracks for home. But we informed them that we had minutes from our Monthly Meetings showing that we were members in good standing, and preferred to pursue our journey and accomplish our important mission. After faithfully commanding the tender plants and young lambs to the fold of God and the word of his grace, we went our way rejoicing that we were counted worthy to be used of God in the salvation of souls, even if it was blended with a little bitter "elder tea."[13]

Rufus Jones gave this account of these early revival days:

This Walnut Ridge revival, the first to occur in a Quaker Meeting, was soon to be repeated, with varying circumstances and methods, in a large number of Quaker communities. Almost at once, meetings in these centres of awakening began to undergo changes. Many young persons now took part in them. Silence gave way to public testimony and prayer. The Scriptures took on a new importance and were early read and interpreted. The old sense of awe and restraint gave place to an era of freedom and spontaneity, and still greater changes were behind. Many, quite naturally, opposed all that was happening. The old ways were praised and commended and the dangers of innovation were proclaimed, but nothing stemmed the current--the old order changed and the new came on apace.[14]

Change was causing tension in many Friends meetings. Yet, most Friends were well aware of the century of separation. The foundational doctrines of the Quaker understanding of the Christian faith were being theologically wrestled with anew and afresh, thanks primarily to Joseph Gurney. But change was not nearly as evident in theology as it was in the *expression* of theology, the forms and practices of the faith. New life could not be denied, however, and most of the yearly meetings sympathetic to Gurney sought to nurture and direct or contain the revivalistic fervor.

In 1867 Indiana Yearly Meeting reinstated the General Meetings of the first Quaker generation. These large meetings were for "teaching, for discussion of central truths and practices, and for outreaching evangelistic work."[15] This work was carried on under the guidance of a joint committee of the yearly meeting and its quarterly meetings. The chairman of this committee was Daniel Hill, who later became the editor of *The Messenger of Peace* and of *The Christian Worker*. The General Meetings or "threshing meetings" were accepted by all Gurneyite yearly meetings, reaching Kansas in 1872, the same year that yearly meeting was established. Ohio, New York, North Carolina, Western, and New England had already welcomed the format of such gatherings.

In 1871 New York Yearly Meeting was "led into a lively desire for a return to the zeal and earnestness of Friends in the early period of their history," and appointed a committee to hold General Meetings as the way opened for the promotion of that objective.[16]

The General Meetings also spread to Iowa in 1872. This was the "first official movement by the church in the direction of holding revival meetings."[17]

> The subject of holding General Meetings within our limits was brought before us. . . .it was thought the time had come for the meeting to engage in such work, by setting apart a committee to arrange for and have oversight of General Meetings for worship and the dissemination of the principles of the Christian religion. . . . An earnest concern was felt that all such meetings be held strictly in the order of our religious society.[18]

The biggest statement illustrating the newness of spiritual vitality in the Midwest was the establishment of *The Christian Worker* in 1871. The *Friends' Review* was not challenging the static nature of the quietistic heritage enough for Friends in the Midwest, and they found a new mouthpiece to support the new forms and methods of the revival era.

The *Worker* would network the revival leaders and the yearly meetings on the frontier and stimulate them through teaching, information, and news of the progress of the revival. The *Review* and the *Worker* would tend toward divergent paths. The *Review* sought to remain intentionally "Quaker," but Daniel Hill, the new editor of the *Worker*, sought a more "Christian" focus encouraging fellowship with other evangelical denominations.

Early Calls
for a Conference

Faced with the excitement of revivalism and the growing diversity among Friends, Western Yearly Meeting in 1870 proposed a general council of all yearly meetings. The following minute was attached to Western Yearly Meeting's epistle and sent to all corresponding yearly meetings.

> This meeting has been introduced into a desire for a more perfect union among the different Yearly Meetings in Europe and America.
>
> There are many departments of Christian labor of common interest that call for united counsel. Some of these are the education of our youth; the publication of books and tracts, and the general diffusion of knowledge by the press; the civilization and Christianization of the Indian tribes, and of missionary work at home and in foreign lands; the distribution of the Holy Scriptures at home and abroad; the more practical and effectual recognition of the principles of peace by Christian professors and by civilized nations; and the determination of such questions as may be of common interest and concern the general welfare.
>
> We apprehend that a General Council, composed of representatives appointed by the several Yearly Meetings,

would have a harmonizing and uniting effect upon our common society, and render the whole and its parts, more mutually supportive of each other, where conclusions and recommendations shall only be advisory in their nature.

Should this proposition meet with general approval, we would suggest that the first meeting be held in the city of New York, on Second-day after the close of Canada Yearly Meeting, in the year 1872.

We desire that the Divine Will may influence and control our counsels in the determination of this important measure, and that what is done may hasten the work of our common Lord and Savior, and honor His church in the earth.[1]

That same year during the yearly meeting sessions of Baltimore, consideration was given to the minute sent from Western Yearly Meeting. Baltimore encouraged Friends to give prayerful thought to such a concern.

The following Report upon the proposition from Western Yearly Meeting was read, carefully considered, and fully united with by this Meeting, and we commend this subject to the prayerful consideration of Friends everywhere, that if it be the Lord's will that such a Conference be held, that the way may open for its assembling.[2]

The following is the report by Baltimore Yearly Meeting's committee which was considering Western Yearly Meeting's proposition. This committee's reflections give real insight to the strong-felt need to gather for such a conference.

The committee appointed to consider the proposition from Western Yearly Meeting, apprehend that co-operation in Christian work is probably on as good a basis in its present form as the nature of the case will admit of; and the other part of the proposition, "to determine such questions as may be of common interest, and concern the general welfare," is hardly, in our judgment, definite enough to warrant such an appointment.

The committee believes, however, that there are periods in the history of the Church when it is called upon to reaffirm its doctrines, testimonies, and mission. In this day of awakened religious interest and inquiry among our own members, and others who are being drawn to us in various sections; in the multiplication of Yearly Meetings, and the rapid increase of membership in some parts, we believe that the time is not too far distant when a General Conference of the Yearly Meetings of this Continent, and of London and Dublin, would be desirable to reaffirm the Doctrines, Testimonies, and Mission of the Religious Society of Friends; and without infringing upon the authority and independence of the several Yearly Meetings in their respective limits, consider subjects which effect our common membership and welfare.

We believe that such a Council, composed of delegates appointed under the promptings, and held under the authority, of Him who is "Head over all things relating to the Church," would bind us more closely together as one people, and strengthen us as a Church.[3]

Though Western was prophetic in nature, it was Baltimore that was asking the more direct questions. Baltimore was clear about the current conditions of the Society. However, both yearly meetings were considering the future of the Society. Could old wineskins contain new wine without bursting? Did the organizational ability of the Church as held by Friends have the flexibility for revival and diversity? As change grew more and more apparent on the frontier, would the common denominator still be present to unite Friends from London to Kansas?

London Yearly Meeting, which usually had given leadership to the Society and which also had sought to be the peacemaker during many rifts within the yearly meetings in America, chose not to participate in such a conference. The "weighty influence" of London was probably the greatest single factor why the conference was not held.

The following communications have been received from the Western Yearly Meeting, and from that of Baltimore, in reference to a Conference of Representatives of Yearly Meetings proposed to be held in America in 1872. This Meeting, whilst feeling a lively interest in all that affects the welfare of the members of our religious Society everywhere, and appreciating the brotherly confidence which has led to the communications, does not see its way to join in the proposed Conference.[4]

The possibility of a general conference was kept very much alive in the thoughts of Friends over the next few years, particularly in Western Yearly Meeting. During its annual sessions in 1875 and after receiving an epistle from Iowa Yearly Meeting about the "long continued absence of correspondence with Philadelphia Yearly Meeting,"[5] Western recorded their sympathy about "the sorrowful and injurious isolation of that Yearly Meeting."[6] Perhaps this renewed their interest in conferencing, because the next discussion centered around considering such a conference again. During this dialogue members present from at least seven other yearly meetings gave encouragement to the opinion that such a conference, if proposed, might meet with general approval. The following minute was then adopted with a hearty approval.

> On the reading of the correspondence from the several Yearly Meetings, this meeting has been again introduced into prayerful and fraternal interest and sympathy for all that bear our name, and especially for the Yearly Meetings on the American Continent. We are impressed, as on previous occasions, with the necessity of a General Conference by delegates from the several Yearly Meetings, to take into consideration and endeavor to reach conclusions upon such subjects as concern the general welfare of our Society; to meet at such time and place as may be agreed upon during the course of its consideration by the several Yearly Meetings.[7]

This minute was appended to all the outgoing epistles. Although the emphasis was directed toward the yearly meetings of North America, once again no support was received from London, which was regularly sending traveling ministers to America with certificates of ministry and minutes. The response was once again insufficient. But the idea of such a conference remained alive, just waiting until the pressure of diversity necessitated such a gathering shortly down the road.

Cast of
Characters

4

Joseph Bevan Braithwaite
(1818-1905)

Dr. James C. Thomas spoke to me with great urgency, saying that it was very important that something should be done. I at last told him that I felt it a very solemn thing, and could not venture to undertake to do anything; but that if they could arrange for Dr. Rhoads to assist me, he and I would, in great fear and very prayerfully, yield ourselves to make the attempt, on the understanding that it was to be a simple compilation from accredited documents, principally our Book of Discipline, etc.[1]

Such were the humble words of Joseph Bevan Braithwaite in a letter to a friend describing his thoughts about the Richmond Declaration of Faith. As one of the six representatives to the Richmond Conference from London Yearly Meeting, the writing of the Declaration would be the high point of his fifth and final visit to the United States and American Quakerism. Now at the age of 69 and considered a spiritual giant of London Friends in the tradition of Joseph John Gurney, he still hoped for a solid and bright future for the Society of Friends.

Joseph Bevan was born the son of Isaac and Anna Braithwaite of Kendal, England, in 1818. He was one of a set of twins who were last born in the family of nine children. The Braithwaite Quaker heritage goes all the way back to the days of George Fox. The richness of that tradition reached high ground with both of Joseph's parents diligent in the ministry and faithful in the nurture of a Christian atmosphere in their home. Isaac and Anna were two of many English Friends who journeyed to America with evangelical Quaker views in the early 1800s.

Anna, particularly, added coals to the fires of the American Quaker Separation of 1827-28. In response to the teaching of Elias Hicks, Anna traveled among the American yearly meetings. Thomas Shillitoe recorded the following about Anna in his journal:

> When Anna Braithwaite arrived in America, they saw a woman of striking appearance and address, whose eloquence attracted the admiration of the young, but whose doctrines were clearly opposed to the new teachings. She strongly emphasized the divinity of Christ and the need for His atonement, and urged upon her hearers the necessity of a change of heart.[2]

In 1823 shortly after Joseph's fifth birthday, his oldest sister penned this letter to her mother while she was in America:

> Bevan continues his fondness for hearing the reading of the Bible, and one day lately, when we were smiling about what trades the boys would like to be when they grew up, Bevan said with great earnestness, "But I will be a preacher."[3]

The decade of the 1830s would be a pivotal time for Joseph Bevan Braithwaite and his future with Friends. The hunger for evangelical nourishment and the fear of Hicksism spreading in England placed Joseph's parents, Isaac and Anna Braithwaite, together in supportive fellowship with others in England. Most notable of these was Isaac Crewdson, a brother of W. D. Crewdson who married Deborah, Isaac Braithwaite's sister.

In 1834 Isaac Crewdson, a recorded minister of Manchester Meeting and Lancashire Quarterly Meeting, published his writing, *A Beacon to the Society of Friends*. Crewdson's brochure was a defense against the views of Elias Hicks, which had the possibility of influence in England. In the early 1800s English Quakerism had two schools of thought. Joseph John Gurney, Elizabeth Fry, Hannah Backhouse, and Anna Braithwaite were clear evangelical teachers who seemed to interest the younger Friends more than the silent meetings or older preachers. John Barclay, George and Ann Jones, Sarah Lynes Grubb, and Thomas

Shillitoe were exponents of the more mystical approach. And some prominent ministers, such as John and Joseph Pease, Samuel Tuke, and Stephen Grellet, seemed to occupy a middle position, being claimed by both parties.

Fearing Hicks' influence on the more mystical Quakers and, thus, forseeing a weakening of evangelical Quakerism, Crewdson seized the extreme passages of sermons and writings of the farmer from Jericho, New York, and forcefully attacked them in his *Beacon*.

Crewdson's extreme view on the Scriptures resulted in much debate through tract writing on both sides in the next few years. At the London Yearly Meeting sessions in 1835, the issue arose and a committee of thirteen, including J. J. Gurney, was appointed to restore unity in Lancashire Quarterly Meeting.

As a result Isaac Crewdson resigned his membership from Friends in 1836 and influenced about three hundred Friends to join him. This separation and unsettledness in the Society caused much upheaval in the Isaac Braithwaite family. Joseph wrote in his *Reminiscences*:

> In 1834 our relative Isaac Crewdson, who lived at Manchester, published *The Beacon*, a book which consisted principally of free criticisms of passages from the sermons and publications of Elias Hicks. . . . This at once gave rise to an earnest controversy into which my dear Father threw himself, with the simplicity which distinquished his character, by printing a letter to Isaac Crewdson (supporting his views), in the composition of which my brother Charles and I assisted, but the publication of which was greatly regretted by my dear Mother, who was absent at the time. . . . Largely as a result of this controversy my beloved brother Isaac and my sister Anna were thrown under the influence of the late Baptist Noel and my dear brother became a clergy man, and my brother Foster and sister Caroline also withdrew from the Society, leaving my brother Charles and myself the only members of the family who remained with Friends. All this was a great trial to my dear Father and Mother.[4]

Joseph Bevan got involved in the controversy, although somewhat anonymously, by writing some letters criticizing the Society. The controversy, however, did get him involved in researching the writings of early Friends. His student years provided an opportunity for him to be a Bible scholar and a "great student of the Church Fathers."[5]

In 1838 Joseph wrote out his resolutions, though he was uncertain of his place in the outward Church. Among these resolutions were the following:

> I must pray earnestly that my motives may be purified and I must strive after practical faith.
>
> Know myself, my own corruptions, temptations and inward hardness of heart. Know and remember these things that I may think humbly of myself and live in humble confidence upon my Savior.
>
> I must rise early. Six o'clock in the morning. . . . I propose to adhere to the following order of studies: 2nd day morning—Greek and Latin alternately, etc.[6]

In 1840 J. B. Braithwaite came to London to complete his legal education and, therefore, attended the London Yearly Meeting sessions. Shortly after his arrival in London, he was on the point of undergoing the rite of baptism and resigning his membership. "But," he wrote, "I thought it only right to attend the yearly meeting throughout, and to form my own independent judgment."[7]

Joseph continued:

> I listened with an open mind to all that passed, whilst I was at the same time writing a pamphlet explaining my views in opposition to Friends. The attendance of the Yearly Meeting deeply impressed me, and I was gradually brought to the conclusion that I must cast in my lot amongst Friends.[8]

After the yearly meeting sessions, Joseph made a public avowal of the change and expressed his regret at the part he played in the late controversy. He was to commit himself faithfully to Friends for the next sixty years. In the year 1844 he was recorded to serve in the public ministry of the Gospel by his monthly meeting of Westminster in London. In the meantime he also fulfilled his requirements as a lawyer and gained considerable eminence in his career in the years ahead.

The next major event in Joseph's life occurred in 1849 when he was selected to edit the *Memoirs of Joseph John Gurney*, who had died in 1847.

> Perhaps nothing could be mentioned which would show
> more clearly the estimation in which Bevan Braithwaite,
> while still a young man, was held, and the confidence in
> his spiritual insight and tact, than the fact that at the early
> age of thirty-two he was chosen to write the life of Joseph
> John Gurney.[9]

In the summer of 1851 J. B. Braithwaite and Martha Gillett were married. This supportive marriage relationship would prove to be a great asset to the future work and ministry of Joseph Bevan.

One other spiritual tension helped to shape the life, ministry, and convictions of Jospeh Bevan Braithwaite. After the stormy sessions of London Yearly Meeting in 1836, and due to the solid orthodoxy of Joseph John Gurney, greater emphasis on the Bible and Christ's atoning death was made by English Friends. As this emphasis grew, a small group (in Manchester again) led by David Duncan sought more liberty of thought among Friends. Duncan openly challenged the strong evangelical position of English Friends:

> The position taken up at present by the so-called
> "Evangelical" Friends of the Bible, is fatal to all spiritual
> life, and all faith in God and truth; it reduces men to
> slavery of mind and spirit; it openly preaches that God may
> have revealed Himself to the writers of the Old and New
> Testaments, but that we cannot, and do not, expect such a
> revelation. This is to shut God out from the world.[10]

In 1870 a committee from the yearly meeting was appointed to counsel Duncan and a few like-minded Friends in Manchester. Joseph B. Braithwaite was the elder of that committee which eventually recommended the disownment of Duncan for "denying the authority of the Bible and the Deity of Jesus Christ."[11]

Thirteen Friends, some who claimed an immediate approach and saw no need of Christ at all, resigned their membership and set up another meeting which continued for only a few years. However, a monthly publication, *The Manchester Friend*, was published for a couple of years. But the challenge of free religious thought was subdued in what became known as the "Manchester Heresy," and Joseph found himself in the thick of it.

Joseph Bevan made five visits to America and gave significant spiritual leadership to both sides of the Atlantic. He journeyed to the United States in 1865, in 1876, in 1878, in 1884, and in 1887. Because

Braithwaite was seen as a distinctly leading influence in the direct Gurney succession, the characteristic Quaker attitudes toward ministry and worship were also taught and therefore preserved among Friends.

It is also important to note that J. B. Braithwaite had great appreciation for the entire ecumenical Church. In 1869 he became a member of the Committee of the British and Foreign Bible Society. He was also glad whenever he found a point of contact with members of the Episcopal and Roman Catholic Churches. One of his close friends was the English missionary to Africa, Dr. Livingstone. Livingstone stayed at the Braithwaite home several times. After his stay in England in 1856-58, Livingstone's family moved to a house close to the Braithwaites so they could support his wife and children while he was in Africa.

When J. Bevan Braithwaite traveled to Richmond, Indiana, in 1887, he was indeed a very "weighty" Friend. His struggle with Quakerism in his early years and his ensuing commitment made him authentic. His disciplined Christian life and his scholarly abilities made him a leader. His long-term relationship with London Yearly Meeting and his association with others in the Universal Church increased his vision of the Gospel. He was prepared, in many ways, for one of his finest hours—the Richmond Conference of 1887.

William Nicholson
(1826-1899) and
Timothy Nicholson
(1828-1924)

Josiah and Anna White Nicholson were a part of a rich Quaker tradition. Four of their five sons, including William and Timothy, were to take prominent places in the Society in the years to come.

We enter the family history about the year 1660 when Edmund and Elizabeth Nicholson came from Cumberland, England, to Massachusetts. After Edmund died, Elizabeth and her two oldest sons, Christopher and Joseph, were heavily persecuted as Quakers in a Puritan colony.

Like other Friends who moved to other colonies as a result of persecution, the Nicholsons journeyed to the Albemarle settlements in North Carolina, shortly before the visit of George Fox and William Edmundson in 1671. "The first marriage certificate recorded in the records of the North Carolina Friends was that of Christopher Nicholson and Ann Atwood."[1]

Thomas Nicholson, a well-known minister among Friends in the 1700s, was the grandson of this Christopher Nicholson. Thomas was said to be "an able minister of the gospel—furnished with a good understanding, and sound judgment, and was zealous for good order and for the peace of the church and for the maintenance of the testimony of truth."[2]

Josiah Nicholson, the grandson of Thomas, was the father of William, born Nov. 9, 1826; Timothy, born Nov. 2, 1828; Josiah, born in 1831; John, born in 1833; and George, who was born in 1835 but died in 1855. Included in this home were three other children, Elizabeth, Rachel and Thomas. They were Anna's children by the deceased William Robinson.

WILLIAM

As a very pious and conscientious youth, William received his childhood education close to home at the Friends Academy in Belvidere, North Carolina. He later attended Friends School at Providence, Rhode Island, where he established a fine record for good scholarship and character.

William then stayed at this school to teach before returning to North Carolina to teach at the New Garden Boarding School (now Guilford College). After attending the University of Pennsylvania, he was graduated in 1850 as a doctor of medicine.

William found his practice as a physician to be a great tool for ministry, while during the Civil War many Friends suffered persecution, even bodily, because of their opposition to the war, their abhorrence of slavery, and their favor of the Union cause.

William found himself involved in politics as he began in the Civil War by visiting President Jefferson Davis and pleading for Friends and others conscientiously opposed to all war. After the war he was elected a member of the State Contitutional Convention, where he exercised much influence on behalf of liberty of conscience and exemption from military service.

As a result of the request of President Grant for Friends to get involved with the Indian policy on the plains, the Associated Executive Committee of Friends on Indian Affairs was organized in 1869 at Damascus, Ohio. This committee was composed of representatives of nine Orthodox yearly meetings. In 1870 Dr. Nicholson was appointed as the committee's first General Agent, to live in the field, to oversee the entire work, and to be a source of accurate information.

After moving his family to Lawrence, Kansas, and developing great executive ability, the United States government appointed William to serve as Superintendent of the Central Division. This division included about 20,000 Native Americans who were experiencing conflicts with the settlers. He carried out this position with great wisdom and efficiency until 1878. William was even elected a member of the Kansas Legislature in 1870.

Most of all, William was a faithful Friend. In 1865 he was recorded as a minister by North Carolina Friends. In 1872 Kansas Yearly Meeting was established, having been set off by Indiana Friends. William was the first clerk and was reappointed each year until he moved to southern California in 1888, where he continued to give good leadership to Pasadena Friends until his death in 1899.

He is noted among Friends for two primary areas of leadership in the last half of the nineteeth century: 1) He wrote with clarity, depth, and conviction, providing a good theological basis for the revival period among Friends. 2) He championed the cause of conferencing among Friends by representing Kansas Yearly Meeting at both the Richmond Conference in 1887 and the follow-up conference in Indianapolis in 1892. He first wrote of the need for a central body of delegates from yearly meetings back in 1880 when the *Friends' Review* published a series of articles entitled "Serious Thoughts for Serious Friends."

TIMOTHY

Timothy also attended the Friends Academy three miles from his home in North Carolina. Like his brother before him, he also traveled to Rhode Island to the Friends School at Providence. Here Timothy's life would be greatly broadened, not only by the education, but by the association of many Friends who became close friends with Timothy even though their homes were widely separated by geography.

Returning to North Carolina, Timothy was eager to help his father on the farm. But another of his father's dreams would need him more. The little country academy was declining rapidly and was in need of a teacher. Josiah Nicholson, a leading member of the academy board, requested that his son of twenty years take responsibility. Although he wanted to be a farmer, Timothy made an excellent schoolmaster.

In 1854 Timothy married Sarah W. Newby and in the next year they journeyed to Haverford, Pennsylvania, where Timothy was to be the head of a new preparatory school near the college. While they were there, they received a good taste of Philadelphia Quakerism as members of Radnor Monthly Meeting.

In 1860 it was on to Richmond, Indiana, for the Nicholsons, as Quakers everywhere, felt the tension of the war. Timothy lived there until his death on September 15, 1924, at the age of almost 96. He and his brother John owned and operated the Nicholson Book Store.

For the remaining years of his life, Timothy would gain much respect for his career as a bookseller, his humanitarian efforts through the state of Indiana, and his service as a solid Quaker elder in the life of

Indiana Yearly Meeting. Rufus Jones wrote:

> Timothy Nicholson has exhibited the traits and qualities of
> mind and heart that have characterized the best Quaker
> reformers of the past. He has had a clear vision of what
> ought to be done; he has been actuated by the Spirit of the
> Master; he has been free from selfishness or self-seeking;
> he has never known when he was defeated; and he has
> worked in fine cooperation with others.[3]

In 1867 Indiana Yearly Meeting appointed a committee of six, of
which Timothy was one, to "organize a system for the reformation of
juvenile offenders and the improvement of prison discipline."[4] In 1870
this committee saw to it that the Reformatory School for Boys was
established in Plainfield, Indiana.

In 1871 the committee petitioned the Indiana Legislature calling for a
board with authority to inspect and watch over the prisons,
reformatories, and benevolent institutions of the state. Finally, in 1889
the committee's request was served as the Board of State Charities was
established to improve the deplorable conditions of prisons and jails.
Timothy Nicholson was a member of that board from its inception
until 1908. Alexander Johnson, the first Secretary of the Indiana Board
of State Charities, said: "It is an moderate estimate of Timothy
Nicholson's work and influence to say that for fifty years he has been,
in all matters of charity and correction, the wisest, strongest, and most
useful citizen in the state."[5]

Errol Elliot is convinced that Timothy Nicholson was one of many
Friends who "were simply not being fashioned by the times; they were
changing the social conditions, and non-Friends in the leadership of the
state were made keenly aware of it."[6]

Timothy Nicholson was also quite active in furthering the temperance
movement.

> He stood staunchly by the women in their crusade,
> assisting them in their meetings on the street in front of
> the saloons. Gospel temperance meetings led by the noted
> anti-liquor evangelists of that day were frequently held in
> the city and Timothy Nicholson was at the head of them.[7]

In 1898 the Indiana Anti-Saloon League was organized and Timothy
was elected its first president, and he remained in that position for over

twenty-three years.

Timothy also served as a member of the Board of Trustees for Earlham College for forty-nine years. He served among Friends in many capacities: a member of the Permanent Board of Indiana Yearly Meeting for sixty years, clerk of Whitewater Monthly Meeting for twelve years, clerk of the Yearly Meeting Body of Ministry and Oversight for twenty-one years, secretary of the Yearly Meeting Book and Tract Committee for thirty-five years, and presiding clerk of the Yearly Meeting for eight years beginning when he was 76 years old.

Timothy had a concern for many years to have a general meeting for all the yearly meetings. The yearly meetings had gathered on behalf of Indians, education, peace, and missions. But a common discipline for all the yearly meetings was the goal. As early as 1866 Timothy was clerk of a committee established by Indiana Yearly Meeting to consider the first suggestion of a uniform discipline. The committee's conclusions were that it was not the right time.

But Timothy himself recorded the formulation of Indiana's concern in 1886:

> During the Indiana Yearly Meeting in 1886, I invited, of the ministers attending the Yearly Meeting, one from each of five other Yearly Meetings and Francis W. Thomas of our own, to take supper at our house one evening; and at the table I introduced the subject of a General Conference of the Yearly Meetings. I briefly advocated and expressed the conviction that this was the time for Indiana Yearly Meeting to take the lead in the matter. Barnabas Hobbs of Western Yearly Meeting, which under his leadership had twice proposed such a Conference, ably supported what I had said; all the others agreed and we requested Francis W. Thomas to introduce the subject the next day to the Meeting.[8]

Timothy was selected as chairman of the Indiana delegation which made the arrangements for the conference. His vision and holistic approach to the Quaker faith cannot be underestimated!

David B. Updegraff
(1830-1894)

Mount Pleasant, Ohio, a small town near the West Virginia border, was the location of the yearly meeting house of Ohio Yearly Meeting, which was set off by Baltimore Yearly Meeting in 1813. This yearly meeting house was the site of two disastrous separations which Ohio Yearly Meeting experienced. In 1828 Hicksites and the Orthodox Friends, nearly even forces numerically, divided the Ohio Yearly Meeting Quaker inheritance. And during the annual sessions of 1854, the Orthodox body itself separated. This time the Wilburite, or conservative body, was larger than the Gurneyite, or evangelical body.

David Brainerd Updegraff was born in 1830 in Mount Pleasant of Quaker parents who were much engulfed in the turbulent Ohio Yearly Meeting waters. David Updegraff's Mennonite ancestors joined the Society of Friends late in the 1600s. His father, David Benjamin Updegraff, was a businessman and a farmer in Mount Pleasant and an elder in Short Creek Monthly Meeting. David's mother, Rebecca Taylor Updegraff, also came of Quaker stock. She married David Benjamin in 1812, was recorded as a Friends minister, and began traveling in the ministry in 1826. As a matter of fact, Rebecca T. Updegraff was one of the visiting ministers at the 1860 Indiana Yearly Meeting sessions who called for the appointment of the special evening meeting for youth which ingnited the revivalism period for Quakers in the 1860s, 1870s, and 1880s.

David Brainerd Updegraff, appropriately named after the well-known missionary and prayer David Brainerd, was the youngest of eight children. After receiving his education in the local Ohio schools, he journeyed east in 1851 to Philadelphia where he attended Haverford College. Here, though he only stayed for one year, he met Dougan Clark, who was to become a life-long friend.

In 1852 he returned to Mount Pleasant, married Rebecca Price, and settled down as a businessman and a farmer. After the separation of 1854, he sided with the Wilburite force until after his conversion experience in 1860, when he united with the Gurneyite Short Creek Meeting.

Allen Jay wrote of the first time he met David Updegraff. Allen was granted a minute from his own monthly meeting to attend Ohio Yearly Meeting at Mount Pleasant in 1859. He met David at the home of David's grandmother, Ann Taylor. She introduced him to Allen by saying, "This is my grandson, David Updegraff. He is not doing what he ought to in the Lord's work."[1] And Allen wrote the following in his autobiography: "It was not long after this that he gave himself to the Lord and entered upon the work that made him such a pioneer in the church."[2]

Charles G. Finney, the great revivalist, was an intimate friend of the Updegraff family. Therefore, the revival spirit was nurtured in David's home. In 1860 the Mount Pleasant Methodist Church was holding a series of revival meetings, and it was then that David was converted at the age of 30. "I was converted through and through, and I knew it. I was free as a bird. Justified by faith, I had peace with God."[3]

Updegraff's next powerful spiritual experience occurred while John S. Inskip, the first president of the National Association for the Promotion of Holiness, was staying in his home. This experience of instant sanctification would provide the basis for his future theological framework. Updegraff recorded: "Instantly I felt the melting and refining fire of God permeate my whole being. . . I was deeply conscious of the presence of God within me, and of His sanctifying work."[4]

His recording as a Friends minister in 1872 would lead him into many controversial days ahead with leadership in Ohio Yearly Meeting and contact with Friends outside of his own yearly meeting. These controversies would center around the development of his four-fold gospel: 1) conversion or "justification," 2) "sanctification," the holiness doctrine, 3) the imminent Second Coming of Christ, and 4) faith healing.[5]

In 1877 Walter Robson, an English Friend, visited several of the

American yearly meetings. He recorded these words about David Updegraff: "David Updegraff is looked on as one of the finest ministers in America. . .[6] and "glad to see the most wonderful Quaker preacher in the United States come into meeting, David Updegraff of Mount Pleasant, Ohio."[7] But it was also during these years that Updegraff was building his theological basis for his teaching of justification and sanctification.

Through his leadership in Ohio Yearly Meeting, the Meeting of Ministers and Elders drew up a minute to "repudiate the so-called doctrine of 'Inner Light,' or 'the gift of a portion of the Holy Spirit in the soul of every man,' as dangerous, unsound, and unscriptural."[8]

Updegraff wrote articles for the *Friends' Review* and *The Christian Worker*, and also preached boldly to emphasize his position.

Updegraff's position on instantaneous sanctification, as well as his forceful use of revival techniques initiated by Finney, such as the "altar of prayer," "mourner's bench," "testifying," and "singing," etc. was not going unchecked, even out further west. Joel Bean, the clerk of Iowa Yearly Meeting and a member of West Branch Monthly Meeting, responded with no support for Updegraff's ministry when he left the West Branch Meeting in "confusion" after a series of evangelistic meetings.[9] And after preaching for one and a half hours during the 1877 Kansas Yearly Meeting sessions, Updegraff met with opposition during a devotional meeting. Walter Robson recorded it this way:

A painful scene was meanwhile enacted downstairs at the devotional meeting. A minister (Cyrus Harvey) loudly declaring against D.U. and his teaching and at last a recorded minister (a woman) went to him and said--"we read of a deceiver and an antichrist and thou art the man."[10]

From Henry Hartshorne of Philadelphia, David Updegraff received this critique:

After going through all of Western Yearly Meeting, attending all of its devotional meetings, and attending a large meeting at Spiceland and several at Indianapolis, and lastly three or four days at Indiana Yearly Meeting, there was nothing which seemed to me impossible to reconcile with the essential principles of the early Friends and the precedents and principles of religious work and worship in the New Testament, until I was present at the two meetings in the meetinghouse at Richmond on 7th and 1st day evenings:—the one mainly conducted by J. Henry Douglas and the other by thyself. I was not there during the whole of the former—but was until just before the close of the latter. Now, my dear Friend, I am bound to say, candidly; that *that was not a Quaker meeting*, in any sense except only that it was conducted by members of the Society of Friends, and in a Friends' meeting house. No precedent for any like it can be found in any history or biography of the days or successors of George Fox; and the *method* of personal leadership, *dictation*, urgency of individual *pressure*—calling out for *expression*,—to say nothing of the *maximum* of *singing* and *minimum* of *silence*—was diametrically *opposite* to that characterizing the early Friends; and *irreconcilable* with the *fundamental principles*.[11]

Updegraff's greatest controversy was yet to come. He and his followers began to preach a much more literal view of the scriptures. This is when David began to teach the scriptural obligation to practice the ordinances, especially water baptism. In 1882 while he was visiting in Philadelphia, David was water baptized by the pastor of the Berean Baptist Church.

In 1885 Ohio Yearly Meeting, greatly influenced by the man and his experiences, "refused to make it a disciplinary matter for a minister to participate in or advocate the necessity of the outward ordinances."[12] But while Updegraff believed that he was simply expressing the freedom that Quakers should have on such matters, the rest of the Orthodox yearly meetings became greatly disturbed. This was probably the single most important factor of the calling of the Richmond Conference in 1887.

In 1887 Updegraff started *The Friends' Expositor* with himself as editor and publisher. He used it as a vehicle for presenting his beliefs over the next few years.

Updegraff passed away on May 23, 1894, and two days later Dougan Clark preached at his funeral service at the Ohio Yearly Meetinghouse in Mount Pleasant.[13] And at Updegraff's memorial service during the Ohio Yearly Meeting sessions of that same year, Dougan Clark was water baptized by John Pennington in the yearly meetinghouse.[14]

Allen Jay (1831-1910)

Probably more than any other Friend, Allen Jay's life represents the best of American Quakerism in the last half of the nineteenth century. He was raised in a godly Quaker home, and he brought much strength, solidity, and balance to the revival movement among Friends in the 1860s, 1870s, 1880s, and 1890s.

Timothy Nicholson said of his contemporary Allen Jay:

> During all of these years in both the Five Years Meeting and Indiana Yearly Meeting and in his own Monthly and Quarterly Meetings, Allen Jay was ever recognized and honored as a wise spiritual leader without a superior.[1]

And Rufus Jones simply said of this man: "He was, I think, the most deeply loved Friend of our generation."[2]

Allen Jay was born in Miami County, Ohio, about thirteen miles north of Dayton. His parents, Isaac Jay (1811-1880) and Rhoda (Cooper) Jay (1813-1894), had grown up in the Miami Valley. In the heritage of both families of his parents, one will find a richness of faithful Quakerism. Born on October 11, 1831, he was the oldest of five children of the loving Jay parents. He had three brothers, Milton, Walter Denny, and Abijah, and one sister, Mary Jay Baldwin.

After his father faced and overcame a serious illness, family worship

(Bible reading and vocal prayer) became a regular part of the life of his home. And Isaac Jay was recorded in 1850 as a minister and over the next thirty years visited all of the American Orthodox yearly meetings except one.

But prior to his father's commitment to family worship, Allen had had a deep conversion experience at the age of thirteen. After a meeting for worship when a traveling minister had spoken to his condition, Allen found a place where he could be entirely alone, and, contrary to the tradition of outward forms in which he was educated, Allen knelt and prayed out loud. He recorded in his autobiography:

> After supper I went out into the orchard and sat down to pray. I wanted to kneel down and offer prayer, but my training was such that I felt that none but those called to public prayer should kneel down. . . Now I was impressed that I should open my mouth and speak out the burden of my soul. But here again my education was such that I was afraid to speak words unless called to public ministry. We had been told we could pray as well by thinking as by speaking. . . The burden was so great that I went back and fell on my knees and broke out in vocal expression, confessing my sins and asking God to forgive. Joy came to my soul. Sweet peace filled my heart.[3]

When you combine his early religious experiences with the home activities of family worship and the overnight visitation of many well-known, traveling ministers, such as Benjamin Seebohm, you can appreciate and understand the influential Quaker Allen came to be. His early years also included experience of the Underground Railroad and a much-loved education in the meetinghouse near his home.

In 1850 the Jay family moved to Marion, Indiana, and in the next year he began attending the Friends' Boarding School (now Earlham College) in Richmond. In 1853 he transferred to a new Friends' Boarding School at Farmers' Institute, near Lafayette. He also attended college for a short time at Antioch College, Ohio, while he lived with his uncle and aunt, Eli and Mahalah Jay.

It was while he attended Farmers' Institute that he met Martha Sleeper, who would be his wife for forty-five years. After marriage, Allen and Martha moved to Greenfield, Indiana, where they both taught school and lived for fifteen years. During this time five children were born; the two oldest died in infancy. Also, it was here at Greenfield Monthly Meeting that both Allen and Martha were appointed to eldership at the young age of 30 years, which indicates that the members regarded them as living blameless lives and having mature judgment on spiritual matters.

Late in the 1850's, Allen was a leading figure in the opening of a First-day school. He taught a class that met each First-day afternoon the whole year round. In giving leadership to the young people, Allen grew deeply in his own spiritual life.

> It was while working with those young people that I first offered vocal prayer in public. I felt the need of it. Sometimes the spirit of prayer would come upon us, and several of the members of the class would engage in prayer. This revival influence was finally felt in the academy, and several of the young people at times were heard in prayer during the morning devotions at the opening of the school. . . Thus, in a quiet way, in this little Quaker community out by itself on the prairie, during the years 1859 and 1860, began this wave of revival work that a few years later began to spread abroad over our branch of the Church in various places. . . .[4]

In the fall of 1868 Allen Jay was called to succeed Joseph Moore, who was called to the presidency of Earlham College, as the Superintendent for the Baltimore Association. The Baltimore Association was organized in 1865 to assist and advise Friends of the southern states in the plight following the war. The association sought to organize and re-establish Friends schools and First-day schools.

Thus, Allen Jay's life of service and ministry deepened. He led in the repair of the building and equipment of the New Garden Boarding School, but also helped establish new monthly meetings and Sunday Schools wherever possible. Allen's leadership was valuable in assisting North Carolina Friends to rebuild their meetings spiritually, which helped to connect up North Carolina to the Quaker revivalism of the West.

To add to his giving and receiving of the Quaker breadth, Allen and his family journeyed to Rhode Island in 1877. Here they spent four years as members of New England Yearly Meeting, while Allen was treasurer for the Friends Boarding School at Providence.

Then in 1881 Allen returned to Indiana where he devoted the remainder of his life to the building up of Earlham College. He was superintendent and treasurer, but also served as solicitor, trustee, member of the board of managers, and involved with various other committees and programs of the college.

This was his basis for the remainder of his ministry among the Society of Friends. Not only was he faithful to the college—getting it out of debt, seeing enrollment increase and new buildings built and the endowment fund increased about six hundred percent—but also he served in great ways as a traveling minister and one of the founders of the Five Years Meeting. He traveled in most of the American Orthodox yearly meetings, including New York and California, as well as overseas to visit Friends in Great Britain and Norway. He was well respected as a wise and steady minister by all of the yearly meetings he attended.

If there was a single person in whom the Quaker Revivalism Movement in the last half of the nineteenth century could best be represented, Allen Jay would be that person. He died in 1910, but not before he had left a valuable written pilgrimage of his life and Quakerism in his autobiography.

In closing this sketch on Allen Jay, two quotations from his autobiography give a look at this balanced, steady, and wise leader. Written early in the twentieth century, the quotations reveal Allen's appreciation of his Quaker heritage and his depth of commitment to the breadth of Quakerism.

In reviewing his conversion experience of the 1840s, he wrote:

> But after threescore and ten years, having seen the results of the ministry of that day, which directed our thoughts to the Spirit of God and urged us to listen to His voice as He called us to follow Him, and comparing it with the dogmatic and superficial teaching of some of the present day, who point us to their own experience in spiritual things, I am ready to say that our father's ministry produced men and women of ability and Christian character which I sometimes fear are not produced by the methods of the modern revivalist.[5]

And while he was involved in the early days of revivalism in North Carolina, he always sought to be sensitive to the concerns of all Friends:

> I do not believe the cause of Christ is advanced by pushing in innovations or change of practice faster than the weight and religious sentiment of the meeting is able to go. For if this is done separations are sometimes brought about and bitter feelings are engendered and things said and done that are contrary to the spirit of the Master.[6]

John Henry Douglas
(1832-1919)

During the last half of the nineteenth century, a new movement among Orthodox Friends was being realized. This movement had two dimensions to it: 1) The American religious scene was experiencing revival. This revivalism affected the Society of Friends. 2) The country was experiencing a societal and cultural expansion of westward movement on the frontier from East to Midwest to West. Friends were a part of this great migration.

These two movements overlapped a great deal into one movement. The pilgrimages of many Quaker leaders could be traced to help understand this movement. However, no one manifests this East to West and Orthodox to Revivalism Movement better than John Henry Douglas.

John Henry Douglas' birthplace and burial place embrace the continental United States. He was born in Fairfield, Maine, on November 27, 1832. Three days short of his 87th birthday and 3,300 miles away, he died in Whittier, California, on November 24, 1919.

Through the careful training of his godly Quaker parents, John Henry developed a deep consciousness and reverence for sacred things. Even as a young boy he sensed visitations by the Holy Spirit. However, the meetings for worship that he attended with his family, which included his brother Robert William, did not speak to his spiritual condition. He was educated in St. Albans and Hartland Academy and then studied for three more years at Friends' School in Providence, Rhode Island.

When John was nineteen, he made a visit to relatives in Ohio. This was a very important trip in his life for two reasons. While enroute to Ohio on the ocean between Maine and New York, the ship on which he was a passenger was overtaken by a severe storm. Here he had his first decisive Christian experience. He wrote in his memorandum:

> Great fear came over me, I was not prepared to meet God. In my distress I called upon the Lord as best I could. I confessed my sins and my undone condition, and some way, I could not understand, my trouble was at an end, and glorious peace came rushing into my soul.[1]

This trip to Ohio was also important because Ohio was soon to become his home and the place where he met his wife. In 1853 John moved to this mideastern state and in 1856 married Miriam Carter, who would be his wife for the next sixty-three years. Over the next few years John Henry farmed, taught in a country school, and traveled the countryside preaching and visiting homes with the Gospel. In 1858 John Henry was recorded as a minister of the Gospel by Dover Monthly Meeting of Indiana Yearly Meeting.

John was involved with the single most significant event for Friends in the revival period. This development occurred at the Indiana Yearly Meeting sessions in 1860. He was one who gathered with Charles and Rhoda Coffin, Murray Shipley, and others to pray and discuss in the Coffin home. He participated in the evening meeting during the yearly meeting sessions that this small group had called for and where more than one thousand attended. He was a part of the younger Friends who met with Sybil Jones back in the Coffin home after the annual sessions concluded.

Revival was on the way for Orthodox Friends, especially for those who were heading westward, and John Henry Douglas found himself right in the middle of it! During the next three decades, John Henry traveled a great deal in the ministry. He did evangelistic, missionary work among Friends, and other denominations as well, in England, Scotland, and the continent of Europe.

In 1866 John Henry was asked to be a resource person for the women of Indiana Yearly Meeting as they chartered the Women's Home Missionary Association. In 1867 the Peace Association of Friends in America was organized, and John Henry was appointed its first General Secretary.

John Henry was also quite interested in education for Friends youth. In 1871, as a leading Friend, he was very instrumental in raising funds for the development of Wilmington College in Ohio. He then served as president of the college's board of managers for twelve years.

Throughout his fifty years of ministry, John Henry widely traveled the United States visiting yearly meetings and preaching whenever and wherever he had opportunity. He was "evangelical" as he preached the necessity of conversion through confession and repentence. And he was a part of the Revival and Holiness Movement as he called for Christians to experience the baptism of the Holy Spirit as subsequent to conversion. In his own experience, even after becoming a Christian, John Henry continued to sense an inner conflict of a spirit of rebellion which was against the spirit of willingness to do the Lord's work. After crying out to God for deliverance, he had an instant and complete victory as he experienced newness of life through the power of the indwelling Christ. This victory, in many denominations and among some evangelical Quakers, was known as sanctification. In some respects, the emphasis of this Holiness Movement was on perfection. The possibility of sanctification as a second definite experience to empower the believer was an effort to be loyal to George Fox's doctrine of perfection.

It would be important to mention some of the other ingredients of John Henry's evangelical theology. His ministry was of the evangelistic type, but through it all he gave definite teaching on the fundamental doctrines of the New Testament, such as salvation through the atoning blood of Christ, His resurrection, the coming of the Holy Spirit on the day of Pentecost, the absolute necessity of the new birth and the baptism of the Holy Spirit as a preparation for effective ministry, the Second Coming of Christ, the day of judgment, the reward of the righteous and the doom of the finally impenitent.

In 1877 Walter Robson, an English Quaker, visited American Friends for a four-month period. Robson gives many accounts of John Henry's ministry in Indiana, Western, and Iowa yearly meetings. The flavor of Robson's journal reveals John Henry Douglas as a powerful preacher and leader in the evangelical Friends movement. Robson recorded one meeting for worship at Indiana Yearly Meeting in 1877 where a revival service took place. This was a new experience for the Quaker from the other side of the Atlantic.

I gave Hannah Whitall Smith my arm and we hurried off to the Friends Meetinghouse where a scene of indescribable

solemnity was being acted "an altar of prayer." Friends old
and young, smart and quite plain, kneeling in rows,
sometimes quite still, often ejaculating short earnest prayer
for a baptism of the Holy Ghost, some praising God with a
loud voice that their prayers were answered. Dear David
Updegraff and John Henry Douglas quietly moving about
among the kneeling throng, sometimes in prayer
themselves and at others, quietly whispering words of
comfort or counsel. I never realized such agonizing in
prayer before. It was a scene never to be forgotten.[2]

But the holiness theme of sanctification in the revivalism movement
was not the single aspect by which John Henry would most be
remembered. In 1886 John Henry became the first superintendent of
Iowa Yearly Meeting. His influence the next four years in Iowa was
very great, primarily through his evangelistic work and his
unapologetic support of the pastoral system. John Henry saw a great
need among the meetings for follow-up for many newly converted
Friends. When he came to Iowa, only a few pastors were receiving any
financial support. When he left in 1890 almost fifty pastors were
partially or fully supported. His justification, of course, was that these
pastors were merely being "relieved as much as possible from business
so that his whole time may be devoted to the need of the church and the
field around him."[3]

Then it was on to Oregon for John Henry. After pastoring the
Newberg Meeting, John Henry was named head of the Evangelistic and
Church Extension Board in 1893, the same year when Iowa officially
set off Oregon as its own yearly meeting.

California Yearly Meeting was officially organized in March of 1895.
John Henry's influence on the cutting edge of this religious movement
continued as he assumed the post of Superintendent of the Evangelistic,
Pastoral, and Church Extension Board of the new yearly meeting. He
also served for a time as pastor of the Long Beach Monthly Meeting.
"His dynamic leadership had a profound effect upon California Yearly
Meeting, molding it in the pattern of the Great Awakening."[4]

After living his last ten years in Whittier, John Henry passed away.
The words from his memorial in the California Yearly Meeting minutes
give a great tribute to his life and ministry:

He seemed to realize that as George Fox and other reformers
were raised up just when they were for a special service in
the cause of Christ, so he was also called to rescue his

people from a deadly error that would lead them out of usefulness as a vital gospel agency. This vision was clear, and he set himself to be obedient to it. . . . His ministry was vigorous and aggressive, and literally hundreds accepted Christ under his earnest appeal. During his life he saw the church rescued from its deadly formalism and brought into a vital relation with the Great Head of the Church.[5]

Mary Whitall Thomas
(1836-1888)

Mary Whitall Thomas was born in Germantown, Pennsylvania, one of the first communities in Pennsylvania which had a strong Quaker flavor. Germantown Friends Meeting will be remembered as the first Quaker meeting which minuted its testimony of equality by challenging the slavery system. In 1688 Germantown Friends sent a protest against the holding of slaves to Philadelphia Yearly Meeting. That protest was the beginning of a long struggle for Friends seeking consistency in terms of the testimony of equality. Equality among women in the late 1800s was a strong theme in the life of Mary Whitall Thomas as a Quaker minister and a feminist. It is amazing to see the strength of such a tradition for peace, righteousness, or justice from generation to generation.

Mary was born on February 24, 1836, the youngest of the four children of John Mickle and Mary Tatum Whitall. Mary's oldest sister was Hannah, born on February 7, 1832. Next was her sister Sarah (or Sally as she was affectionately called by her family) who was born on March 7, 1833. James, the third child and only boy, was born on September 3, 1834. The four children, close in age, grew up together in many ways in the Whitall household. Another child, John, born after Mary, died in infancy at the age of two and one-half. John's death sent Mary's parents into deep grief, and it is no wonder that Mary's sweetest recollections of her childhood reminiscences are of remembering her father's tender care for his children when they were sick.

> So thoroughly delightful was it to be taken up out of our
> beds at night, and soothed to sleep again by him, that it
> would have sometimes been almost a temptation to have
> feigned a little indisposition, if it had not been for our
> father's utter and uncompromising contempt for all shams,
> which he impressed so strongly upon all around him, that
> we would not have dared to brave his unqualified
> displeasure. Although he was most indulgent and
> affectionate in every way, and careful to put no restrictions
> upon our freedom that were unnecessary, yet we well
> understood that we must be truthful and honorable, "open
> and above board," as he used to say, if we wanted to meet
> the approval of him whom we loved so well.[1]

When the Quaker testimonies, particularly equality in this
instance, are combined with a strong and healthy family life, it is no
wonder that girls and boys who grew up in such homes became strong
women and men for the cause of Christ. Such was the case with this
Whitall home. Hannah, the oldest child of the family, became a well-
known Christian author during the last half of the nineteenth century.
She wrote many books but will be especially remembered for her
classic, *The Christian's Secret to a Happy Life.*

Hannah disrupted the tradition of this tight Quaker family by
resigning her membership from the Society of Friends in 1859, eight
years after her marriage to Robert Pearsall Smith. Hannah and Robert
were intense seekers of the Lord and His Truth, much like Hannah had
been nurtured to be in her early years. After a great deal of study, she
submitted to water baptism at a nearby Baptist church and partook in
the outward elements of communion. For several years she was not
welcomed in any of the homes of her family--her parents' home as well
as her siblings' homes. Years later the relationships with her family
were restored, and Hannah was found preaching to and worshipping with
Quakers again during the Holiness Revival years. In the biography that
Hannah wrote in 1879 about her father's life for his grandchildren, *John
M. Whitall: The Story of His Life,* she included many tender words
about their early home life:

> Our parents were not rich, and had to deny us many
> luxeries, but what they did give, was given so heartily and
> with such a genuine expression of desire that it could have

been a great deal more, that we forgot the slim realities, and felt ourselves as rich as the wishes would have made us. . . And poor as we were, there were no happier children in Philadelphia I am sure.[2]

All four children have very fond memories of their early home life and growing up with John and Mary Whitall as parents. However, particularly the girls remembered the strength and encouragement which their father instilled in their hearts. These moving recollections by Mary and Sarah, respectively, suggest that John Whitall was perhaps ahead of his time as a feminist bringing out the best in his daughters.

Our father's return home from his counting room in the evening, was a daily recurring joy to us, and was looked forward to as the brightest time of all. Our little heads were generally to be seen peeping out of the front door every few minutes about the usual time for his return, watching for the first sign of the well beloved face in the distance. Then when he finally arrived, came the shout of childish joy, and plenty of hugs and kisses, and after the first eager question "Where's mother?" had been answered, the next thing was a game of romps, with all of us hanging round him and climbing over him, our cup of happiness full to the brim with his companionship. Then, when the supper bell rang, I can almost see him now, tottering down stairs to the dining-room, with our brother in one arm, and me in the other, and Hannah and Sally hanging on to his coat tails. After supper, came romps again, and then we were carried, and coaxed off to bed, and undressed and "tucked up" by our lovely father-nurse, who thus relieved our dear mother for a little rest after the tender and watchful care she had taken of us all day in his absence. And he would leave us at last to a happy sleep, made all the happier by the consciousness we had of his nightly unuttered but never omitted prayer beside our bed.[3]

We girls knew that our father not only loved us more than any other girls--for all fathers love their own the best--but we knew that he had an especial and individual admiration for each one of us; that he thought we were superior. He had a good opinion of us, and he did not mind showing it. I do not think this made us conceited, for we knew it was only the result of his partial love; and besides, he never spared reproof when it was needed, and it was needed a great deal; but it made us love him with perfect devotion. We

would sometimes, too, hear pleasant and complimentary
things that he said about us to other people; and how our
hearts did leap, not because of the compliments, but
because he thought so of us.[4]

Hannah was married in 1851. Sarah married William H. Nicholson, a medical doctor (but not the brother of Timothy Nicholson) of Linden, New Jersey, in 1855. About six months later Mary married James Carey Thomas of Baltimore, Maryland, on October 31, 1855. He was also a medical doctor. And about one year later, James, the only son, married Mary Cope. Thus all four Whitall children married within the Quaker ranks. This was also a result of their growing up in a strong Quaker home, where the faith of the Religous Society of Friends was obviously considered the clearest expression of the Christian faith.

It was during the early years of her marriage that Mary clearly embraced the Christian faith through commitment in what Hannah called conversion. Each of the Whitall children professed such commitments as young adults, and their father saw these as the fulfillment of the Christian nurture in his home. John Whitall was of the Orthodox tradition of Friends in Philadelphia Yearly Meeting. This can be seen in this letter he wrote to Mary shortly after her conversion:

I hope we are all thankful to our merciful, kind, Heavenly
Father, who has indeed blessed us as a family, and
particularly in giving us a good hope through grace, His
own precious grace in His dear Son, of eternal life. I always
trusted that in His love He would bring my children one
after another into His covenant of life and peace; peace with
Himself through our Lord Jesus Christ, whom to know is
life eternal.[5]

Mary Whitall and James Carey Thomas had eight children, four girls and four boys. The oldest child, born in 1857, was Martha. Martha's life story gives a reflection of the strength of this feminist tradition of the Whitall family. After completion of her secondary education, Martha, with the strong support of her mother, talked her father into allowing her to go on to college. This was an unusual thing for a woman to do in the nineteenth century. She was graduated from Cornell University with Phi Beta Kappa honors in 1877. When she decided that she wanted to go on for more graduate studies, she discovered that women were not eligible for doctorates at that time in America. So Martha travelled overseas to Switzerland and obtained a doctorate summa cum laude from the University of Zurich.

At this time the Orthodox-Gurneyite Quakers of the Philadelphia area wanted a comparable Haverford College education for their daughters. James Carey Thomas was a founding member of the board of directors when Bryn Mawr College opened its doors in 1884. James Rhoads was the first president of the women's institution, and Martha Carey Thomas was the first dean. (From the beginning this college had high academic standards. The only original member of the faculty who did not have a doctorate was Woodrow Wilson, who taught history, economics, and politics while completing his doctorate at Johns Hopkins University.) In 1894 Martha succeeded Rhoads as president. She retired in 1922, but not before she had established Bryn Mawr as the first and finest graduate school for women in America, even with programs leading to a Ph.D. degree. She was a pioneer in education and a feminist well ahead of her time. She grew up in the home of Mary Whitall Thomas, who seemed to be able to combine the best of the women's movement and the Quaker convictions of the Christian faith of her day.

Mary and James lived in Baltimore all of their married life, except for a short term during the Civil War in 1861 when Massachusetts troops were attacked in the streets of Baltimore and the city was placed under martial law. Mary, James, and their family returned to Germantown to live with her parents during the tensions of the war. However, when they did return to Baltimore, their ministries grew more than ever in their home, in medicine, and in the Eutaw Street Friends Meeting. Mary was recorded as a minister in 1871 through Baltimore Yearly Meeting. Mary and James were a part of the Gurney-influenced flavor of the Orthodox Baltimore Yearly Meeting. Their home was always a place of hospitality for traveling Friends, and the relationships built during such times paved the way for the "connectedness" that many Friends had during the later Richmond Conference. James' brother, Richard Thomas (also a medical doctor), was married to Anna Braithwaite, the daughter of Joseph Bevan Braithwaite. Anna wrote a biography on Richard and included many thoughts of his larger family. She wrote this about James and Mary:

> Dr. James C. Thomas, too, was a man of broad outlook and wide culture. As a minister he was remarkable for a variety of subject and freshness of thought. He was a great lover of young men and always attracted them. He had started, years before, a boys' meeting at Light Street on

Sunday afternoons, which was really a Sunday School for
boys, with classes ranging from little tots to grown-up
young men, and with an average attendance of some two or
three hundred. At this time, and until his death in 1897, he
was President of the Baltimore Young Men's Christian
Association. His wife, Mary Whitall Thomas, was also a
very attractive minister. She had a tireless energy and an
eager longing after spiritual blessing that led her to wish to
test for herself every system that seemed to promise more
grace or power. Her heart overflowed with the love of God
and a yearning for souls. She was identified with the work
of the Women's Christian Temperance Union, and had been
almost from the first its President in Maryland. During the
winter 'that Moody spent in Baltimore, she worked most
earnestly among drinking men, and was the means of
reclaiming numbers, so that one of her friends remarked
that it was as much as any man's character was worth to be
seen conversing in the street with Mary Thomas. She and
her husband were then in the prime of their power.[6]

Ecumenical in nature as most Gurneyite Quakers were, Mary Thomas
was pulled into many ministries where her gift of leadership could be
thus utilized. As well as serving with the W.C.T.U. of Maryland, she
was also a founding member of the Young Women's Christian
Association of Baltimore. She also served on the boards of McCall
Mission and the Baltimore Orphan Asylum.

Another aspect of her ministry included the writing of a number of
tracts. Among these were written "Foundation Stones" in 1875 and
"Was Baptism by Water Commanded by the Lord Jesus Christ?" in
1883. At the time that she was a delegate, along with her husband,
from Baltimore Yearly Meeting to the Richmond Conference in 1887,
she was also the clerk of the Maryland Women's Yearly Meeting.
During these years, Mary was also in declining health, much of which
she kept from her husband. Anna Braithwaite Thomas gave this account
of the closing months of Mary's life:

That autumn the first General Conference of Friends was
held at Richmond, Indiana. A delegation from London
Yearly Meeting attended it, amongst them my father and
my uncle George Gillet. In our Baltimore delegation were
James C. and Mary W. Thomas, and Mary S. Thomas.
(Mary Snowden Thomas was a sister of James and she later
married Isaac Braithwaite, a cousin of Anna.) Our delegates
returned with glowing descriptions of the Conference.

Every "Orthodox" Yearly Meeting of Friends in the world had been represented and there had been the greatest good feeling and spiritual power and blessing. A Declaration of Faith had been drawn up and adopted, and nothing remained but for each Yearly Meeting to endorse it, and thus a check would be speedily put upon growing divergencies in faith and practice, and a wondrous unity would be produced.

We had time to think it over, for a month elapsed between their return and the holding of our Yearly Meeting. Indiana, the largest and strongest Yearly Meeting in America, the one we had always looked up to and followed, was held, and it adopted the Declaration with enthuasiasm. Then came our own Yearly Meeting. Leading Friends from Indiana, New York, etc., were in attendance, besides nearly all of the English and Irish delegates to the Conference. It was a wonderful time, unique perhaps in the history of little Baltimore. All our work was going on so well, and to our great joy, a net increase of sixty-nine was reported, bringing our total membership up to 907. . .

Another matter of great interest was the Incorporating of the Yearly Meeting, whereby it became legally qualified to hold property, etc., and in the re-adjustment that was then made, women were given an equal place upon its Permanent Board, and as Presiding Clerks, etc. Mary Whitall Thomas was then Clerk of the Women's Meeting and had acted throughout the Sessions, many of them held jointly, with all her accustomed ability. It was recalled afterwards that once or twice she had spoken as though her work was over, and all had noted the power and tenderness of her prayers on more than one occasion.

The record Yearly Meeting was over--the Meetinghouse which for a week had hummed and overflowed with busy life was silent and empty, our visitors departed and life returned to its accustomed channels. But the very next day we learned the overwhelming news that sister Mary was ill with a malignant disease, and that fatal consequences were feared. It was too true; only once again did she cross the threshold of that Meeting-house where for a quarter of a century hers had been such a pervading influence. From the day that she admitted her illness her strength failed rapidly, and eight months later, on July 2, 1888, she passed away.[7]

58

"The Interchange" of Baltimore gave this conclusion to the report of those 1887 Baltimore Yearly Meeting sessions:

> At the close of the meeting, one of the clerks (Mary W. Thomas) prayed most impressively for a blessing to rest upon all the Yearly Meetings, that Friends everywhere might be equipped for the work of the Lord and be as one body in the faith and hope of the Gospel, a prayer with which it was evident that every earnest Christian soul present united.[8]

Esther Gordon Frame
(1840-1920)

Esther preached to them with a power that held that company of men and women of all grades of society perfectly entranced. It was a new and strange thing for a Quaker woman to preach, and especially on the street. Her message to them was a most wonderful one, and before the sermon was ended there were as many as 500 gathered at that street meeting, and they stood there quietly the full two hours that the meeting lasted, and all that time there was perfect order and quiet reigned.[1]

Esther Gordon and Nathan Frame (1835-1914) met each other while attending an academy in Salem, Iowa, in the 1850s. Their families were pioneers along the frontier in Iowa. They both had Quaker influence in their families' backgrounds, but both of them encountered Christ through the ministry of Methodists. Many of Nathan's father's ancestors were Friends. Esther's mother's family were Mendenhalls, and her Grandmother Mendenhall was an elder among the Quakers.

Esther was born on August 10, 1840, in Wayne County, Indiana. Her conversion experience occurred while she was a young girl in Thorntown, Indiana. She had been attending the Friends school one mile outside of town but started attending the Methodist Academy in Thorntown because it was closer to home. It was then that she committed her life to Christ at an altar call during a series of meetings.

She recalled: "The Lord laid his hand on me to preach when I was not more than seven years old. . .As soon as I was converted the weight of souls came upon me. I did not know what it meant then, but in my teens God gave me souls while He was preparing me for the ministry—all through the years between the time of my marriage and my conversion."[2]

> In the beautiful spring days, at noon time, it was my delight to assemble my playmates around me, and standing on an old stump, or in the "high gallery" seat in the old meetinghouse, and preach to them, and I was not satisfied until I had made them weep at some story I had told them. I believe the Lord *even* then was preparing me for my work in the ministry, but I did not know it.[3]

Nathan's conversion came shortly after he met Esther and primarily through her influence and the meetings of her Methodist Church in Salem. Nathan walked Esther to her home after an evening church gathering on the second night of protracted meetings. Upon their arrival, he knelt down in her house and began to pray. Soon after his conversion, Nathan and Esther were married in 1856.

He then joined the Methodist Episcopal Church of which Esther was already a member. Nathan was licensed to exhort by the Methodists, and Esther was also much involved as "she was a great favorite and very successful in winning souls to Christ at this time."[4] But Esther sensed God's calling to a preaching ministry. The Methodists did not recognize and ordain women ministers at that time, so Esther began to attend the Quaker Meeting at Salem. Nathan hesitated. "I had little knowledge of Friends as a church," he wrote, "and I had no desire to have it increased."[5] He also hesitated because, at first, he felt uncomfortable with Esther's call to preach, not due to an interpretation of the scriptures, but because he didn't want his wife criticized and ridiculed as a rare "woman preacher".

But preach she would! She and Nathan joined Friends largely for the freedom for Esther to be fully recognized in ministry. Two painful experiences occurred during these early years of their marriage. During the winter of 1858-59 their first-born child died while only a few months old. Though two more children, daughters Tassie and Corrinne, were born into their home, such grief did greatly affect the course of their lives and ministries.

One bleak December night, when the fierce storm and wind
with cold hands was shaking the windows and the cold
snow was drifting around our dwelling, the messenger had
come, the blue eyes opened wide and gave a loving look
into the mother's face as she pressed him to her heart and
the spirit had flown from the delicate little clay tenement.

A few intimate friends went with us from the vacant home
to the cemetery and we laid our first born away to sleep
until the resurrection morning. When we returned to our
home we felt as millions have done before—that the home
had been robbed of one of its brightest jewels.[6]

The other painful experience was the bittersweet departure from the
Methodists. Nathan and Esther applied for letters of transfer to
hopefully take their membership from the Methodist Church to the
Religious Society of Friends. (The Friends, however, did not receive
letters from other denominations at that time.) Esther recorded this
breaking away from the church which had nurtured her during the early
years of her spiritual journey.

I now determined to become a Friend, though the
Methodists were pleading with me to come back to them,
and the minister who had given us the letters, and the
presiding elder, besought me to put my letter back in the
church, and said they would give me license to preach in
their district, but they could not *ordain* me.

At the close of the Conference year another minister was
sent to Salem, and he came to see me and asked for my
letter. I gave it to him, and he said to me after reading it:
"Now, Sister Frame, let me keep the letter, and you come
back to the church; all are ready to welcome you." I told
him that I was called to preach and that Friends granted
women the same privilege in the church that they allowed
man. I shall not soon forget the look of contempt he gave
me as he replied, "It is all nonsense to think a woman is
called to preach." He sealed it then; I felt the chain was
severed and I must seek a home somewhere else and asked
him to hand me back my letter.[7]

In 1867 Esther and Nathan made their way back to Indiana where they
would begin an extensive traveling ministry together, not simply
among Friends, but as evangelists having meetings among various

churches and denominations throughout the United States. Esther would have health struggles even from these days as a younger adult, but she would always seek to be faithful to the word of the Lord that came to her: "Preach my Gospel!"

After arrival in the area of Richmond, they attended Concord Friends Meeting, West Grove Friends where they became members, and Chester Friends Meeting which was about three miles north of Richmond. Everywhere they worshipped they stirred up new life among the more conservative and what Nathan called the "old-time quiet Friends." When Nathan took a teaching position, they transferred their membership to nearby Dover Friends Meeting where they were recorded as ministers of the Gospel in 1869.

Nathan had a solid ministry in his own right, but Esther was known as the powerful preacher. Walter Robson, an English Friend traveling in the United States in 1877, observed Esther at Ohio Yearly Meeting: "A lady Friend, Esther Frame (very young) spoke for an hour and a half, the most finished wonderful sermon I ever heard, on the words, 'made unto us wisdom, righteousness, sanctification and redemption.'"[8]

Esther made quite a stir wherever she went in several ways during those years of revival. She was a Quaker evangelist. She was a woman preacher. She was one of the first to be considered as a "hireling minister" among Friends when she first received a free will offering. Prior to this, for three and one half years, Nathan and Esther lived off of the sale of their home so they could travel full time in the ministry. Their lives and ministries represent the struggle of the beginnings of the pastoral system among Friends. They felt that Friends suffered because of the lack of support for the ministry and that many of the most able ministers left Friends to join other denominations. They believed that "the ministry in Society of Friends was *hampered*, *hedged* in, and not *properly sustained* by the church."[9]

> Until now I had devoted my time during the winter months to school teaching. Selecting schools in places where there was a Friends meeting, and we thought the Lord would have us work.
>
> Now we felt we must give *all* our time to the work of the Lord. Our financial resources were limited to the little amount that was left from my last winter's school, and we had lived on it during the year and paid house rent. Friends in Indiana Yearly Meeting at this time made no provision for the support of their ministers, except to sometimes

supply them with money to pay their traveling expenses, when a meeting had liberated them to travel in "Truth's Service" away from home, and when they could not pay their own expenses. . .

The men and women who consecrated themselves as Evangelists, and spent their lives in preaching the gospel, in "The Society of Friends," must look for their reward *hereafter*, rather than *here*. While the people to whom they preached, lived in good homes, surrounded with all the comforts, and sometimes the luxuries of life, many of them wealthy.[10]

A couple of quotations from newspapers in communities where Esther ministered give a delightful picture of this woman. Such newspaper articles always spoke of both Esther and Nathan, but they always spoke first and primarily of Esther, "the woman in black." From her ministry in Wilmington, Ohio:

Mrs. Esther Frame is a remarkable woman and wonderful preacher. She is gifted. Her dramatic powers are great. I would not say she acts, for her face is lit up with a truthful and devout soul when she pleads for Jesus, but nature has given her genius, a voice of exquisite sweetness, of thrilling pathos; when she discusses the beauties of heaven you see a surpassing glory; when she pictures the condition of the lost, you walk in Dante's Inferno.[11]

From the Cincinnati Gazette was this account of Esther's ministry in Richmond, Indiana:

Any person familiar with the peculiar manner of worship indulged in by Friends, would be astonished to see the amount of excitement this outpouring of God's Holy Spirit has caused in the membership. . .

A Mrs. Frame, perhaps, is one of the most remarkable preachers in this revival,--tall, graceful, and commanding in appearance, and a voice full of music, she can enchain, and melt into tears an audience sooner, than any person it has ever been our pleasure to hear.

Originally a Methodist, she joined the "Society of Friends," because she conceived she had a mission to perform in the

ministry that she could better accomplish there than
anywhere else. Her success has been remarkable.
Presbyterians, Methodists, and other churches, are now
vieing with each other to have her preach to their
congregations.[12]

When Esther and Nathan Frame and John Henry Douglas joined
Friends for the weekend dedication meetings for their new meetinghouse
near Londonary, Ohio, an independent observer (not a Friend) sent this
report in to the Chillicothe newspaper:

The Quakers have a reserve force that other denominations
fail to recognize, and permit to remain almost useless--
Woman power. . . If no other pulpit efforts were ever made
before the large audience by a woman minister, than the
sermons preached by Esther Frame, it was enough to settle
the question, and establish her claim to the pulpit, in the
minds of all intelligent people. . . As her soft mellow
voice raised and rolled on through the house bringing tears
from old dry eyes like great rain drops, the writer could not
help but think, that if good "Old Paul" had been there, he
would straightway have revised some of his Epistles.[13]

The evangelical ministry of the Frames was ecumenical in nature as
they preached outside of Quaker circles and often pulled several
denominations together for special meetings in various communities. In
community after community Esther broke down the prejudices against
women preachers. In 1877 while preaching during a series of revival
meetings in Hillsboro, Ohio, in which Presbyterians, Methodists,
Baptists, and Episcopalians were all participating, Esther was stricken
with paralysis and fell to the floor. Esther wrote about this experience:

The room was filled with the glory of the Lord, and there
was a light brighter than the midday sun, and the faces of
those around me looked like burnished gold, and appeared
more beautiful than any faces I had ever beheld, and I bathed
in a sea of liquid light, and wave after wave came over me,
and I was in a sea of the Saviour's love, and he appeared to
me. I bowed my head for my crown, and reached my hand
for my harp.

But the Saviour said: "Not now, my child, thy family and
souls call thee back."[14]

Though her health was very fragile throughout her years of ministry, Esther would continue in the traveling with Nathan though in later years she would rest for longer periods in between meetings where they would preach. Toward the end of the nineteenth century they visited Salem, Iowa, once again.

> At Salem Friends meeting is where Esther had given her name more than twenty years ago to become a member of Friends. We had continually to keep *hushing* and *silencing* the crying away down in our hearts as we traversed the streets of the little town. Here we had lived, both of us, when we were boy and girl. Here we had gone to school, here I had been converted, here we had been married, here all our children were born. Here our first born was buried, here we fought the battle of consecrating ourselves to the life of evangelists. From here, with trembling steps, we started out into untried fields, leaving all the loved associations behind. And now, after twenty years of more of toil and battle, is it any marvel that all the ground seemed sacred.

> Dear old home, and dear old *home* meeting, *farewell*. How the shadows of life lengthen as the sun passes beyond the zenith. The power of mind and body grow more feeble as we approach the end.[15]

Nathan died on December 27, 1914, in Washington D.C., and Esther passed away on June 11, 1920, in Texas. Both were buried in Jamestown, Ohio, which was their final home. But somehow home for them was wherever they were living lives of faithfulness—whether in the deep South and Florida, the far West and California, or extensively throughout the Midwest. They were home whenever and wherever they were together, with Christ, in His service.

Benjamin F. Trueblood
(1847-1916)

> It is impossible to set forth the career of this noble man of
> God without touching upon his work as a Christian
> minister and his constructive idealism in the development
> of the Society of Friends. . . . He had a very broad grasp of
> the entire field of American Quakerism. He knew its main
> currents and its back eddies. He was very active in the
> conferences which preceded the establishment of the Five
> Years' Meeting, and was a positive force for large programs
> in the early meetings of that body. In church affairs he was
> a statesman with vision. He combined in his heart a very
> dear love for his own denomination, with the most kindly
> catholicity of spirit toward all other followers of Christ
> who walked beneath different denominational insignia.
>
> --Charles M. Woodman, *The American Friend* [1]

Benjamin Franklin Trueblood was born on November 25, 1847, into
the home of Joshua A. and Esther (Parker) Trueblood of Salem, Indiana.
John Hay, destined to be the great Peace Secretary of State, was also
born in the community, though nine years earlier. In this town was a
little peace society. One wonders the impact it might have had on these
two boys who would become movers and shakers for peace many years
later.

After preparing for college at the Friends Blue River Academy near
Salem, Benjamin went on to Earlham College and was graduated with

the degree of A.B. in 1869. Then he received a master's degree from Earlham. After this schooling, he studied theology for a while and then was recorded as a minister of the Gospel.

After teaching at Penn College in Iowa as a professor of Greek and Latin and marrying Sarah Terrell of Ohio in 1872, Benjamin accepted the position of president of Wilmington College in 1874. He served Wilmington until 1879, but his concern for education on the frontier moved him back to Penn College where he served as president until 1890.

In 1890 Benjamin received the degree of L.L.D. from Iowa State University; and in 1908, Baylor University conferred upon him a similar honor.

Besides knowing Latin and Greek, he was an excellent speaker of French and German, and he could read Italian. Benjamin was a life-long student of philosophy, theology, and politics. Because of this, he "never outgrew the feeling of the college professor or, indeed, of the college student."[2]

After his ministry of education in Iowa, Benjamin traveled for one year in Europe, primarily in France, as a spokesman for the Christian Arbitration and Peace Society of Philadelphia. This prepared him for what would be the remainder of his life's work as he was elected General Secretary of the American Peace Society in May of 1892. For the next twenty-three years he faithfully executed the responsibility of the high office of that society, which was founded in 1828.

As Rufus Jones wrote, Benjamin Trueblood would be a "foremost exponent among Friends of the new way"[3] of peacemaking. This new way was a much more rational approach to peacemaking, and it included meetings for the study and propagation of methods of arbitration and the judicial settlement of international differences.

As Secretary of the American Peace Society, Benjamin was also editor of its organ *The Advocate of Peace*. This ushered him into the realm of writing, and for the next twenty years he would write many editorials, essays, and pamphlets, as well as deliver speeches throughout the nation and around the world. His position would send him to many peace conferences in America and the annual international peace congresses. He also had private conferences with Presidents McKinley, Theodore Roosevelt, Taft, and Wilson and lobbied greatly on Capitol Hill and in the State Department for his convictions about the moral damage of war.

So strong were his peacemaking abilities, that is was said of him at his memorial service: "Especially as a discriminating interpreter of the peace movement he had no equal in America, and probably none in the entire world."[4]

Benjamin Trueblood's commitment to Quaker education was one aspect of his concern for the future of the Society of Friends. As president of Penn College when John Henry Douglas was General Superintendent of Iowa Yearly Meeting, Benjamin was giving leadership while the pastoral system was coming into fruition. After the Richmond Conference, Benjamin received a letter from James E. Rhoads of Philadelphia Yearly Meeting:

> We all look on to note your plan of pastorates. If followed out rigorously, it should effect a rapid growth of the yearly meeting in membership and congregations. The difficult task will be to preserve the freedom of prophesy, and the exercise of spiritual gifts by women. Yet I presume this is not impossible by any means.[5]

Six years later after Benjamin had written an article of the progress of change in the Society, James Rhoads wrote Trueblood another letter:

> I wish I could fully share thy hopeful view about the pastorate system, for I am unable to see how it can fail to destroy the principles upon which worship and ministry among Friends from their origin have been based.[6]

The progressive creativity which Benjamin Trueblood had with the newness in the peace movement was also indicative of his views on the Society. He was a leading exponent of what he called the "New Quakerism." He viewed the break with the established pastoralism of the Church of England and the Puritans by the early Friends as being against "the extreme formalism and empty professionalism of that day." He viewed the idea of Quakerism being "primitive Christianity revived" as referring to the "life and religious activity of the first century, not its forms." He believed that "Quakerism itself became formal in the dark century of 'quietism.' It has now, in the last half of the nineteenth century, broken from that shell--free!"[7] Even more than the new forms, such as the pastoral system, Benjamin was thrilled over the new freedom among Quakers of his day.

This Friend died on October 28, 1916, at New Highlands, Massachusetts, and was laid to rest in Wilmington, Ohio, next to the grave of a son who had died in infancy.

Setting
The Stage

Growing Diversity
and Conflict

Walter Robson, an English Quaker visiting the American yearly meetings in 1877, left an extensive account of his travels in a journal. He came to America at a time when Orthodox Friends in the Midwest were caught up in the revival movement. These Friends were moving into three camps: 1) The first group believed that the revival movement was actually changing the essential truths of Quakerism. This group, representing the conservative position, gave way to some small separations with some Friends feeling kinship with the Wilburites of an earlier generation. 2) The second group was the group very supportive of the newness of the revival movement. Traditional Quakerism, not being understood or appreciated especially by many of the new converts, was disregarded by this group. 3) The last group, perhaps the largest, combined elements of both as the moderate group. They were grateful for the freshness of the spiritual vitality of revivalism, but they sought to find a synthesis with the essentials of traditional Quakerism.[1] The basic questions of this moderate group were: When have you changed the meaning of truth? Or when have you changed the expression of truth?

Walter Robson saw himself as one who sought to support the moderate position and bring the two outside groups together. Two separations occurred in 1877 at the yearly meeting sessions of Western and Iowa with the conservatives withdrawing. The following is an account of a series of General Meetings held at Bear Creek Meeting in Iowa.

> The General Meeting in 1877 followed the previous custom of holding immediately following Quarterly Meeting in Second Month. Benjamin B. Hiatt, now a member of Hartland Meeting, Iowa, and Isom P. Wooton, also of Iowa, had the meetings in charge. . . . During the first two days the meetings were conducted after the usual order, but on Fourth-day morning a change came. A "call" was made by B.B. Hiatt for all those who wished to forsake sin and lead a different life to come to the front seats. About twenty arose at once, some not waiting to reach the aisles stepped over seats, and the "mourners bench" was again introduced into Bear Creek Meeting. Great confusion followed. Some who did not come forward were visited at their seats, where prayer groups were formed. Some in the room were praying, others weeping aloud, some were pleading, and occasionally another would break in with a stanza or two of a hymn. The more conservative Friends, who had been dissatisfied all along with these revolutionary revival methods, and had used their influence to hold it in check, or keep it out, were much hurt by this move. Apparently by common impulse, they left the meeting and began to depart for their homes. As a parting testimony against it, one elderly woman, before taking her departure, standing in front of the "mourners bench," declared that the Society of Friends is now dead. That this action had killed it. This seemed to be an expression of their feelings in general as their subsequent action showed. . . . A revolution had come upon the Friends of Bear Creek and also a separation.[2]

A conference for those members of Bear Creek Quarterly Meeting who were dissatisfied with the new changes in the order of the Church was held in May of 1877. The conference led to the establishment of Bear Creek Conservative Friends Monthly Meeting during the next month. The monthly meeting minutes began with a synopsis of "the present and sorrowful condition of our beloved and once highly favored Society by relapsing into doctrines, forms, and practices which we believe are inconsistent with our principles and profession and detrimental to the religious growth and prosperity of the society."[3]

All three monthly meetings of the Bear Creek Quarterly Meeting—North Branch, Bear Creek, and Summit Grove—participated in the separation. During the yearly meeting sessions in September of that same year, two sets of reports representing two separate quarterly meetings were contributed.

Robson wrote in his journal:

> . . . then began Iowa Yearly Meeting. . . A very painful circumstance has occurred. Bear Creek Quarterly Meeting has sent up two lists of representatives, two sets of Answers to the Queries. The clerk, Joel Bean, said we could receive neither till it was decided which was the right one and it was referred to all the representatives. . . . It soon became clear that a body of over 200 members of Bear Creek Quarterly Meeting have separated and set up a Quarterly Meeting of their own, taking five recorded ministers with them. They separated because they say, Friends have forsaken the old paths, Barclay, etc. They are in short Wilburites. It was finally decided to report to the Yearly Meeting which was the proper list of representatives and to advise the appointing of a committee to visit the Quarterly Meeting, to try and restore, in the spirit of meekness.[4]

The next day Robson, along with other visiting ministers including Stanley Pumphrey, met with representatives of the Friends of Bear Creek. Robson left this account of that meeting.

> We begged them not to complete the separation and spoke very lovingly and earnestly and much prayer was offered. The poor dear Friends took our labours very kindly and we feel we have done our duty, but they replied they had not left us but we were leaving them.[5]

The split was inevitable, and the separated Friends of Bear Creek Quarter set up their own Iowa Yearly Meeting that same week in another building in Oskaloosa. It is interesting to note that one of the visiting ministers in Iowa that year was John Henry Douglas of Indiana Yearly Meeting. He would become the first General Superintendent of the Gurneyite Iowa Yearly Meeting in just a few years.

Robson, John Henry Douglas, and others who attended Iowa Yearly Meeting journeyed to Western Yearly Meeting. They soon discovered that a similar occurrence was taking place as had happened at Iowa Yearly Meeting. Plainfield Quarterly Meeting had two sets of representatives and answers to the queries.

The report of the Committee about the two reports from Plainfield Quarterly Meeting, deciding in favour of the liberal one, was read and a very painful but touching scene followed. Robert Hodson, a dear old Friend, rose and said, "he felt he and his party had no longer any rights or privileges among us," and he invited all, young and old who desired with him to maintain Friends principles in their purity, to withdraw to another place, where they might form a Yearly Meeting. Several earnest appeals were made that they would not separate and especially the clerk—Barnabas Hobbs. . . gave a thrilling appeal, but it was no use and 99 men were counted out of the house. Meanwhile a very similar scene was enacted the other side of the shutters, in the' Women's Yearly Meeting. It was very, very sad.[6]

It was also at these Western Yearly Meeting sessions that Walter Robson mistakenly added fuel to the fire of the "hireling ministers" controversy. During the Meeting on Ministry and Oversight the subject of paying ministers was discussed, and Robson spoke at some length. "Immediately almost, after I had sat down, in true American freedom, Daniel Hill brought pencil and paper and requested me to write down as nearly as possible all that I had said, or at any rate the headings, because he wanted to print it."[7]

Among several other controversial remarks, Robson was quoted in *The Christian Worker* as follows:

. . . when a man, called by the Head of the church to preach his Gospel, gives up his time to it, we have no right to call him a hireling minister, even if he receive one or two thousand dollars. . . . If a minister, full of love to Jesus, and called to the work of the ministry by the Holy Ghost, gives up all his time to the work (be he a Friend, or any other name among Christians) surely it is the church's bounded duty to support him, and if need be, his wife and family too.[8]

Perhaps, without fully realizing it, this English Friend helped to open the door for the pastoral system to take a stronger foothold on the frontier.

The 1870s and 1880s were filled with the spread of new thoughts and forms in worship and ministry among the Society of Friends. The experiential revival period would unfold the need of clarifying theological positions and scriptural interpretations. The interrelatedness of the work of the Holy Spirit, the understanding of the Bible, and the life of the Church would be challenged by leaders of the Friends Revivalism Movement. Particularly, three areas became topics of spiritual and theological debates during these decades culminating, somewhat, at the Richmond Conference of 1887. The diversity of thought and practice in regard to 1) "sanctification", 2) "the ordinances", and 3) "pastoral ministry" provided most of the conflict.

Throughout Orthodox Quakerism, J.J. Gurney had already established an acceptable atmosphere of change, of challenge to the old conservatism. Among Gurneyite Quakerism, however, stood a diversity of leadership who were willing to change, but only to varying degrees.

For example, Henry Hartshorne and James E. Rhoads, Philadelphia Quakers and editors of the *Friends' Review,* encouraged new life in the Society, particularly through the renewal of education. In Philadelphia they were considered "liberal," yet among Orthodox Friends of the Western frontier, they were considered "moderately mild" and even quite resistant to the innovations. Yet, both Hartshorne and Rhoads, through their instrument of the *Review,* sought to openly discuss and dialogue the concerns of the Society to bring hopeful unity and new strength.

In a letter to Dougan Clark, Hartshorne encouraged such openness.

> If any leaders maintain the attitude of not listening to any fraternal suggestion, while at the same time they are manifestly proposing new standards of doctrine (now, that is, among Friends) and new practices,—what hope is there of harmony throughout the Society? This position is no better, toward that end, than that of Philadelphia Yearly Meeting; which initially assumes that nothing is right which has not been said or done in Philadelphia within the last hundred years. The result of such unwillingness to *try to find a place of unity* must be further distractions in the Society. An effort to lead our body into Methodism while retaining another name *may* perhaps succeed with hundreds of members in some places; but it cannot succeed with the whole Society. Breaking up must follow; unless the strength of the body is sufficient to withstand such a strain upon it.[9]

One can continue to gain further insights of disunity in the period in the correspondence between Henry Hartshorne and David B. Updegraff. Again and again, Hartshorne makes his case for his moderate position to Updegraff.

My whole mind, given as if in soliloquy, is about this: David Updegraff is a young man of great natural talent and enthusiasm, who has excellent acquaintance with the Scriptures, earnestness and sincerity, and considerable religious experience,—whose views in regard to worship, preaching and evangelizing work have, so far, been *overmuch influenced by the Methodists with whom he has been associated*, and by the *reaction* from the routine and uniformity which bound up the Society of Friends as with graveclothes some years ago—which reaction, needful as it was, has *gone too far*.[10]

In defending his editorial ,position of the *Friends' Review* to Updegraff, Hartshorne wrote:

Acknowledging the kindness as well as frankness of thy answer to my letter, I must say that it *disappointed* me; in two ways. First, it shows a misunderstanding altogether of *my stand-point*. Secondly, it shows a greater unwillingness than I had hoped for, not only to accept, but even to *consider*, a *suggestion* from a friend and brother. . . . The Friends' Review may do *good* and should be continued; and that, *in order* to do good, it must be *moderate*. This moderation is *not lukewarmness; it is adherance to truth and right, notwithstanding the opposition of extremes*. That is our position; and I believe that I am so situated as to be able to recognize what *are* extreme views and actions, better than *leaders* are, on either hand.[11]

And, once again, Hartshorne has a frank reply to a letter from Updegraff challenging Hartshorne's position.

Just *one word* of thy kind note, last received, I must not, for truth's sake, accept. *I am not on the fence*. Rather, my experience had led me to choose the *middle of the highway*; where I see, on the one hand, some dear old friends laboring with their heavy wagons in *deep roots;* and, on the other, young men moving over the *summer road*, at a speed which is *attractive*, but less safe for themselves and neighbors.

A few years, I think it probably, will bring thee *nearer to the middle of the way*, where, though less smooth, it is *better picked* for lasting through all weathers and seasons, that we may *meet with joy* at the *end of the journey*, and *abound in clarity meanwhile*, is the prayer of thy friend.[12]

Henry Hartshorne and James Rhoads both hoped that through open dialogue, education, and conferencing the Society might make progress and yet avoid lack of unity. In 1883 they proposed a gathering of Friends for such a purpose.

> A Conference of Friends from all our Yearly Meetings is proposed to be held, for loving and prayerful consideration of the present state and best interests of our religious Society, at Richmond or Indianapolis, Ind., 6 mo. 30; just following the meeting of the Educational Association of Friends at Richmond.[13]

The three major areas of concern for Friends which threatened the Society were 1) the "workings of the Spirit" in *sanctification*, 2) the life of "ministry in the Church" concerning *pastors and the hireling ministry*, and 3) the use of the *ordinances*.

The primary Friends leaders who were claiming freedom and innovating change were David B. Updegraff, Luke Woodard, Dougan Clark, John Henry Douglas, Robert William Douglas, Calvin Pritchard, Esther Frame, Nathan Frame, and Benjamin Trueblood.

Allen Jay, Barnabas Hobbs, Timothy Nicholson, William Nicholson, Joseph Moore, and others sought to hold a middle position by nurturing the revival, yet remaining sensitive to the Quaker tradition.

Henry Hartshorne, James Rhoads, J. Bevan Braithwaite, Mary Whitall Thomas, James Carey Thomas, James Wood, and Joel Bean were among those who longed for a fresh awakening among Orthodox Quakers, but remained firmly convinced about Friends historic testimonies and the larger Society.

Sanctification

David B. Updegraff had his "instant sanctification" experience in 1869. During the decade of 1870 he enthusiastically wrote and preached about the validity of this experience, which he believed was intended by God as universal for all believers. The Friends background of the "baptism of the Holy Spirit" and the doctrine of the "Inner Light" would necessarily become focal points of attention.

D.B. Updegraff used the channel of the Meeting of Ministers and Elders of Ohio Yearly Meeting to explicate his ideas. In 1877 that body recorded that it

> ....was brought into deep exercise and travail concerning unsound and mystical views and expositions which appear here and there in certain of our members, in opposition to the plain Scriptural doctrines of man's darkness and deadness in sin by nature, and his redemption therefrom by the Lord Jesus Christ, whose shed blood is the alone means of cleansing the soul from all the guilt of sin; and it was concluded that a non-acceptance of this doctrine is a manifest disqualification for the station of Minister or Elder.[1]

In 1878 this same body reaffirmed this minute and went on to say that they "do not believe there is any Principle or Quality in the soul of man, innate or otherwise, which even rightly used, will ever save a single soul."[2] The minute of 1878 went to declare that the "Holy Spirit is sent to convince the ungodly of sin; who, upon repentence toward God, and faith in Jesus Christ who died for us, are justified by his blood."[3]

But the one sentence which sent shock waves across Quakerdom, was recorded as follows:

> And we repudiate the so-called doctrine of "Inner Light," or "the gift of a portion of the Holy Spirit in the soul of every man," as dangerous, unsound, and unscriptural.[4]

In 1879 the Meeting of Ministers and Elders added another minute, and then all three minutes of the last year were printed with the Ohio Yearly Meeting minutes of 1879. This minute of 1879 was rather lengthy, but here are some excerpts which seek to justify the earlier two minutes.

> It is against an important perversion of Truth that we thus protest, and not for a moment against true doctrine when declared by Fox, Barclay, or by Gurney, who says: "Our Lord Jesus Christ bestows a measure of the enlightening influence of His Spirit on all." . . . In other words, it is to imply that a capacity to receive salvation, is a portion of salvation, and that Light in the heart of Christ, however dim, is actually Christ Himself. . . . there is no "principle" or quality in the soul of man that can ever save him, but that God himself must save sinners. It is a dangerous mysticism which knows no distinction between a Principle or an Influence, and Deity himself, continually confusing the two.[5]

The minute continues with expositions of earlier Friends and extensive Scriptural teaching about the work of the Holy Spirit in the life of the believer. During the same time the Ohio Yearly Meeting of Ministers and Elders were passing their minute in 1879, D.B. Updegraff was communicating his ideas on a broader basis. He wrote an article entitled "The Light Within" for the *Friends' Review* in April of 1879. In it he called for the acceptance of two thoughts.

First, he believed that the doctrine of the Inner Light was dangerous because it "is generally so difficult to be clearly understood"[6] and "it is sadly evident that the original and true views of Friends are confounded and identified with those Socinian and mysticised views which in 1827 swept away more than fifty-thousand members of the Society."[7]

Updegraff continued:

> If there is indeed a "Christ in the soul of every man," who can save him if obeyed, then it is true that we need no longer look to the Christ that died at Jeruselem, but mind the Christ in ourselves. . .[8]

Secondly, in the same article Updegraff expounded on the teaching that "through the Holy Spirit, sanctification is produced in the twinkling of an eye!"[9]

Reaction to David B. Updegraff and Ohio Yearly Meeting was swift. The *Friends' Review* acknowledged that the doctrine of the "Light Within" needs to hold two truths in balance.

> Every great doctrine of Christianity is liable to perversion or misapplication. The truth that Christ not only "died for all," "gave Himself a ransom for all," but also is the "true light which enlighteth every man that cometh into the world," has not escaped such perversion and misapplication.[10]

The editor of the *Review* went on to state that if sanctification in the "twinkling of an eye" meant the "state in which Adam was before he fell" as George Fox believed, taught, and confessed, then nowhere could he find in earlier Friends writings that it was suddenly experienced.[11]

James E. Rhoads closed his editorial by stating that "the discussion of this subject of the Light cannot be profitably pursued further in our columns at present."[12]

Whereas the *Friends' Review* represented Gurneyite thought from Philadelphia, *The Friend* represented Wilburite thought from Philadelphia. The editorial from *The Friend* recognized the Ohio Yearly Meeting minutes as the first time that a body calling themselves Friends officially disclaimed the doctrine of the Inner Light.

> It is as wide a departure from the doctrine of "universal saving Light," as always held by Friends—though in an opposite direction,—as was the heresy of E. Hicks and his followers. . . . Must not the query arise in every fairminded

> Friend, what right have a body of people to pass
> themselves off as Friends, while repudiating one of the
> fundamental and distinquishing doctrines of the gospel, as
> ever held by the Society?[13]

The editorial goes on to criticize London Yearly Meeting for not taking a stand against the Ohio Yearly Meeting minute when a deputation team had recently been sent to Western Yearly Meeting to advise the Conservative Friends who were withdrawing.

> If we remember aright, part of the deputation team sent out
> by London Yearly Meeting last year were in attendance at
> the meeting which issued the last minute. Nothing is said,
> we believe, in the account published of their labors, of any
> opposition to, or disapprobation of, the doctrine contained
> in the minute being manifested by them.[14]

Sure enough, Joesph Bevan Braithwaite was a part of that deputation team visiting Ohio Yearly Meeting in 1878. In a letter to Joseph Taylor of Burlington, New Jersey, Braithwaite wrote in a section underlined as *Strictly Confidential*:

> . . . . David Updegraff called for the reading of a doctrinal
> minute which they made last year with the view of its
> being reaffirmed and ordered to be acted on. This occasioned
> long and desultory discussion, which led to further action.
> David Updegraff has it seems written a paragraph in one of
> the Ohio Newspapers, which another friend, an elder,
> thought fit to answer; one denying the other affirming that
> there is a measure or portion of the Holy Spirit in every
> heart. The friend, who affirmed this, fully admitted that all
> in their natural state are dead and in darkness; but with this
> they were not satisfied. A committee was appointed to draft
> a statement of doctrine to be brought in to the next sitting.
> The subject was brought so awkwardly before the meeting,
> and so much time occupied with the discussion, that way
> did not open for us to say anything; except to point out
> that in England we should have thought such a mode of
> bringing about unity by no means the best; and to suggest
> that anything like personal charges might be avoided. The
> latter hint they acceded to; though, knowing the parties
> interested, it was obviously very difficult. Richard
> Littleboy also tried to say a few calming words. But we
> both came away sad and somewhat discouraged.[15]

Ohio Yearly Meeting's minute sent shock waves through Quakerism. Even John Greenleaf Whittier sent a letter to *The Friend* citing "more regret than surprise" at the extracts of the minutes. He added: "They seem to me an entire abandonment of the one distinctive and root doctrine of our religious Society—that from which it derives all that is peculiar to it in doctrine and testimony, and which alone gives it a right to exist."[16]

The Holiness Movement, which emerged during the last half of the nineteenth century right in step with revivalism, emphasized a "sanctification" with the Holy Spirit as subsequent to the conversion experience. The message was being shared to call Christians to a deeper commitment and a more victorious life. Several Midwestern Friends, such as David B. Updegraff, Luke Woodard, Dougan Clark, and John Henry Douglas, gave this sanctification teaching a place of eminence in their leadership and preaching. They claimed that George Fox proclaimed a theology of "Christian perfection" as a result of the baptism of the Holy Spirit. The primary conflict, however, among Friends seemed to be in regard to the insistence that this sanctification experience was "instantaneous" and "entire."

Luke Woodard published his book *The Morning Star* in 1875. It immediately became a source of contention between the *Friends' Review* and *The Christian Worker*. Henry Hartshorne as the new editor of the *Review* would not print a paper written by David Updegraff concerning Woodard's book. Hartshorne, without even consulting his Committee, rejected Updegraff's paper as "not acceptable" for the pages of the *Review*. "There is, then, no occasion for any defense of the book for *its* sake, or for its author's sake. The only question about argument concerning it in *Friends' Review* is, that of *profit* to *readers*, for *truth's sake*."[17] The primary point of contention to Hartshorne was Updegraff's and Woodard's teaching that "*sanctification is always instantaneous*."

However, there seemed to be more at stake in Hartshorne's mind than just the implications of the doctrinal differences. Hartshorne didn't like these Midwestern Friends holding such leadership authority. Consider this critique of Updegraff in Hartshorne's letter:

> One word or two *fraternally*. For one so *indifferent* to *precedent* and *usage* amongst Friends, thy position seems to me a remarkable one, in regard to the right of a *minister* to *dogmatize*. Is Pope Pius IX right after all,—or is it true that any Yearly Meeting or Quarterly Meeting or Monthly Meeting may put a speaker or writer *above criticism or question*?[18]

Dougan Clark's book of 1878, *The Offices of the Holy Spirit*, stressed further the position of an "entire and instantaneous sanctification" experience. The yearly meetings were forced to dialogue about this question of sanctification, and the season of dogmatizing gained in fervor due to the conflicts.

In April of 1884, John Henry Douglas, David B. Updegraff, and Dougan Clark received a letter from Henry Hartshorne while they were together. Hartshorne took the liberty upon himself to offer some "practical suggestions; based on a good deal of observation and correspondence, i.e., among *Friends*."[19] He listed six points in his letter, covering all of their areas of error that were plaguing the Society. He represented many other Orthodox Friends when he wrote:

> I strongly believe that as things are going on now, the Society of Friends will go to pieces, and much of it will melt amongst other bodies—Methodists, Episcopalians, Presbyterians, Baptists, etc., within a few years. I also believe that you three men, John Henry Douglas, Dougan Clark, and David B. Updegraff, may, under God, *save* the Society from disintegration in our time. How? By *conceding*, promptly, frankly, openly and practically, the six points mentioned.[20]

These six points deserve mentioning because Henry Hartshorne did have a representative view of Quakerism through the *Friends Review.*

1. The Society can not be perpetuated with the use of the ordinances-- "water baptism and the ceremonial supper."
2. The Society can not be perpetuated with "instrumental music in meetings for worship."
3. The Society can not be perpetuated with "individual settled and *paid* pastorates; one man for a congregation."
4. The Society can not be perpetuated with the "repudiation, disuse, or discouragement of silence as a background or preparation" for worship.
5. The Society can not be perpetuated with the "holding and preaching of the doctrine that perfect sanctification is, as a rule, and should always be expected to be, completed all at once, by one Baptism with the Holy Ghost."
6. The Society can not be perpetuated with the "practical acceptance of the special guidance of ministers in their preaching; as to where, when and what they preach, as Friends have always held."[21]

84

Of these six concerns, the three major tensions of the early 1880s were 1) the doctrinal and experiencial questions of sanctification, 2) the practice of the ordinances, and 3) the beginnings of the pastoral system.

The Ordinances

David B. Updegraff was not criticised by other Friends simply because of his views on sanctification and the Inner Light. He holds a unique place in Quaker history as a radical who influenced many Friends to practice the ordinances, particularly water baptism.

After many years of being influenced by leaders from other denominations and coming to his own understanding of the scriptures, Updegraff believed that Friends shouldn't be legalistically against the ordinances. In 1882 while he was visiting in Philadelphia, he asked the Rev. Edgar Levy, the pastor of the Berean Baptist Church who was simply giving Updegraff a tour of the church facilities, if Levy would baptize him.

The next few years of Ohio Yearly Meeting history provide a rare example of how the beliefs and actions of one Friend can influence an entire yearly meeting. Shortly after Updegraff's return to Ohio, some Friends sought to have his standing as a recorded minister dropped by the yearly meeting. But other Friends joined him in challenging Ohio Friends to open up on this issue. Many writings representing the convictions of both sides circulated among the Quakers of Ohio.

Friends from three quarterly meetings in Ohio Yearly Meeting developed a declaration for which they sought approval during the yearly meeting sessions in 1885:

> We feel called up at this time to re-affirm the Scriptural
> views always held by Friends upon the subjects of Baptism
> and the Supper. We believe that the baptism which
> appertains to the present dispensation is that of Christ who
> baptizes His people with the Holy Ghost, and that the true
> Communion is a spiritual partaking of the body and blood
> of Christ by faith. Therefore, no one should be received,
> acknowledged or retained in the position of minister or elder
> among us, who continues to participate in or advocate the
> necessity of the outward rite of Baptism or the Supper.
> Monthly Meetings shall be bound by this rule.[1]

It must be remembered that a lack of understanding and tolerance paved the way for two devastating separations earlier in Ohio Yearly Meeting's history, one in 1828 and the second one in 1854. And now, once again, Friends in the yearly meeting were fairly equally divided over an issue. However, after much discussion, those who opposed the declaration against the use of the ordinances held the majority at a two to one ratio. "The pro-Updegraff faction was small, but very vocal and influential."[2] Tolerance, with the hope of preventing another painful separation, was granted in regard to the ordinances.

Again, all of this must be seen in the context that the Ohio Yearly Meeting to which Updegraff belonged was only one-third (or one-fourth) of the original Quaker pie. In 1828 the separation was a 50-50 ratio of Hicksites and Orthodox Friends. Once again, in 1854 the ratio was 50-50 as the Orthodox divided between the Wilburites and the Gurneyites. To give an example of the narrowing views of the yearly meeting, in 1836 Elisha Bates was disowned by Ohio Yearly Meeting (Orthodox) for simply being water baptized.

In the midst of the tension of this issue, D.B. Updegraff encouraged the yearly meeting in 1885 to be open and tolerant with the use of the ordinances. He argued his position from his interpretations of the New Testament and from the early Quaker leaders' tolerance and, particularly, their challenge not to do things simply for the sake of tradition. Due to his strength as a leader and an articulator, Updegraff was able to prevent the motion re-affirming the traditional Quaker position from being approved.

Ohio's lack of affirmation of the historical position on the ordinances challenged the other American yearly meetings to clarify their positions on this topic. Nine other yearly meetings, in just the following year after Ohio's pivotal decision on tolerance, took action adopting declarations very similar to the one rejected at Ohio. A typical form of this declaration is found in the minutes of Indiana Yearly Meeting:

> We believe it inconsistent for any one to be acknowledged or retained in the position of Minister or Elder among us who continues to participate in or teach the necessity of the outward rite of baptism or the supper.[3]

To be true to this statement, Indiana Yearly Meeting was required to drop Dougan Clark's status as a recorded minister. However, he was permitted to retain his membership. (Dougan Clark was later baptized at the memorial service for David Updegraff at the Ohio Yearly Meeting sessions in 1894.)

Though Updegraff had influence in regard to the ordinances outside of Ohio, the other yearly meetings did not have the strength of such a position on the ordinances, and the affirmations of the historical Quaker position were approved with hardly any dissent. Yet, of all the possible reasons for unsettledness in the Society which led to Indiana's call for a conference in 1886, this issue was foremost.

Updegraff's views were also picked up by the ecumenical community. Henry Hartshorne wrote letters to the editor of two Christian periodicals which exposed Updegraff's views as representing Quakerism.

> *Editors of the Christian Union:*
> Allow me most respectfully to protest against the heading of the letter published in your paper. . . . by D.B. Updegraff, upon "Baptism" as "The Views of a Friend." That heading may easily mislead readers unacquainted with the Society of Friends into the supposition that such views are compatible with its accepted doctrines; whereas they are, upon the subject of Water Baptism, diametrically opposed to all that has been written and taught by its standard authors and preachers since the origin of the Society. . . . While it is true that the author of the letter has not yet withdrawn from membership in the Society, to which he was born, it is safe to say that such an exposition could never have been written by one who was truly a "Friend" by conviction.[4]

Again, in 1885 Hartshorne took it upon himself to clarify to the readers of *The Christian Witness and Advocate* some misconceptions in an editorial on the Quakers and the sacraments. Hartshorne wrote that no yearly meeting proposes to expel members who are baptized with water. . . but, "what has been concluded is that for ministers to hold, teach, and administer the ordinances is so contradictory to the convictions always held and hitherto universally expressed by the Society of Friends."[5] Also, Hartshorne defended Quakers by saying that the "object of the existence of the Society is not to 'make war upon' rites, or anything else, except Satan."[6] To this ecumenical audience, the editor of the *Review* included this comment: "David Updegraff. . .is at full liberty to withdraw from the body with whose standards he has ceased to agree."[7]

David Updegraff did have some opposition in Ohio Yearly Meeting which would follow him all the way to the Richmond Conference. Israel P. Hole, another leader within Ohio, addressed the 1885 Yearly Meeting session in response to Updegraff's position.

Hole's response included the mission of the Society of Friends as teaching the spirituality of the Christian faith, especially from the words of Jesus. Also, Hole realized the need for fellowship with other Friends and warned the yearly meeting that not approving the affirmation might cut Ohio off from the rest of the Society.

In 1886 Hole wrote Timothy Nicholson in regard to the possibility of a Richmond Conference in 1887.

> Upon further prayerful deliberation, I am more and more deeply impressed, that a general conference of all the Yearly Meetings ought to be held, in the near future. Thy thought, of our Society tending toward Congregationalism, unless authority be delegated to a representative Council, is entirely in my line of thought and belief. Just as soon as every church (or society or meeting) becomes an independent organization, then the Society abandons the place, which in the economy of grace she was called into being, to fill. And the mission of the Quaker is ended. This seems to me to be the most favorable time in the history of our society to call and create such a council. Probably, all the Y.M.'s, but Ohio, could agree upon the proper status of the Church, upon the outward ordinances, and the clear and definite utterance of such a body, would be worth much to us, either in reducing our revolutionists to order (which I do not expect can be done) or failing in that, and driven to the necessity of a separation.[8]

Writing to Updegraff in regard to water baptism, Henry Hartshorne called upon Updegraff to renounce his position for the sake of the Society:

It is, in my opinion, deeply to be regretted that one who has had such experience, and can write and speak so well, should still have among his "human imperfections" what I regard as (why not speak the truth in love?) the folly of dropping down from Quakerism to water baptism and the greater, and with more difficulty supposed innocent of folly of attempting to lead the Society of Friends to such a collapse;—instead of, in obvious consistency, leaving the Society when he has abandoned its principles, known to be *now* held by 12 of 12 Yearly Meetings, and by half of the membership of his own. . . . It's all a sad mistake, brother;—come back, come back, come back![9]

The Pastoral System

The rise of the pastoral system was also one of the three main issues which was causing change and turmoil in the Society. If Gurney can possibly be blamed for this departure from tradition, it would only be on the basis that Gurney encouraged intentional, systematic discipleship as essential for Christian growth. This prompted regular family devotions, holding special meetings for Bible study, and teaching children to pray out loud,—all the things which would possibly prevent a "Hicksite heresy" from occurring again and all the things which opened the door for the revival period among Orthodox Friends.

With the revival gathering momentum, the General Meetings developing more organization through a "chairman," and the frontier Friends' meetings desperately in need of traveling ministers, Benjamin Trueblood got the debate started in 1872 through the mouthpiece of the recently developed *Christian Worker.* "What is the duty of the Church in the support of the Gospel?" was his opening sentence in an article entitled "Ministers' Wages."[1]

"I conclude, therefore, that to be 'a good minister of Jesus Christ, nourished up in the words of faith and of good doctrine,' one must give himself prayerfully, studiously, continuously to the work."[2] Thus wrote Trueblood as he sought to establish a difference between the hireling ministry, where someone might be in it only for the money, and liberating . people to minister by helping them with financial support, for which he found a Biblical basis. "Preaching for money is certainly a thing wholly different from receiving support after an entire surrender of time and talent to the service of the Lord."[3]

In the next issue of the *Worker*, Trueblood developed his argument: "It seems to me, that the work of every true minister is two-fold, aggressive warfare upon the world and the internal work of church-edification."[4]

> The Society of Friends, failing to give ample support to those whom it recognized as ambassadors for Christ, and thus compelling them to devote but a small fraction of their time to direct labor in the Gospel, lost in great measure its original aggressive spirit. Attempting to live in its own atmosphere, it was fast consuming its oxygen. The ministry of Friends was for many years confined almost entirely to its own borders: even the traveling ministers preached almost exclusively within the Church. I insist upon it, that the carrying out of the aggressive principle of the Gospel requires the cash. In attempting to make the Gospel free to ourselves we have almost failed to give it to the world at large.[5]

Nothing immediately earthshaking resulted from Trueblood's articles. Perhaps the reaction was not stronger simply because Trueblood was only twenty-four years old and just fresh from theological training. But he was prophetic as he examined some of the failures of the past and called Friends to a vision of the future. A definite seed was planted among the meetings along the frontier, the subscribers to *The Christian Worker*.

The debate quieted somewhat with the exception of Iowa Yearly Meeting, which stopped making a statement against the paid ministry in 1874. In the following year Iowa made a provision for pastors in a revision of the *Book of Discipline*.

Also, it was claimed that there were some individual efforts during the years 1870-1874 for a paid pastoral service. Robert Douglas, Luke Woodard, and Nathan and Esther Frame later claimed to experiment with paid service as evangelists doing follow-up ministry after revival campaigns.

In 1877 Walter Robson, the traveling minister from London Yearly Meeting, gave opportunity in his remarks at Western Yearly Meeting for Daniel Hill, the editor of *The Christian Worker*, to state that Robson made a "difference between preaching for pay and being paid for preaching."[6]

Robson was quoted as saying:

> If a man undertake the solemn responsibility of the
> Ministry of the Gospel, *not* from the constraining love of
> Christ, but as a means of getting a living then *he* is truly a
> "hireling minister."
>
> But when a man, called by the Head of the church to preach
> his Gospel, gives up all his time to it, we have no right to
> call him a hireling minister, even if he receive one or two
> thousand dollars.
>
> If a minister, full of love to Jesus, and called to the work of
> the ministry *by the Holy Spirit*, gives up all his time to
> the work (be he a Friend, or any other name among
> Christians), surely it is the church's bounded duty to
> support him, and if need be, his wife and family too.[7]

It was John Henry Douglas and Iowa Yearly Meeting that sought to
systematically develop a pastoral system to meet the growing need of
discipling new converts on the frontier. Richard Wood in *Quaker
Worship in North America* concludes that Midwestern Gurneyite
Quakers had four options to meet this growing need:

> First, they could cut back on evangelism to a level of being
> able to incorporate the new members effectively. Second,
> they could withhold membership and use non-Quietistic
> methods for the new converts in separate meetings until the
> new attenders were ready for the higher standard of
> membership. Third, they could encourage the yearly
> meetings to be more systematic in distributing ministers,
> provide more support and advice, and give financial support
> at time for ministry. The fourth option was to encourage
> each meeting to have the desire and ability to support a paid
> pastor.[8]

John Henry Douglas had pastored in Muncie, Indiana, in 1878. Des
Moines, Iowa, of Iowa Yearly Meeting had Isom P. Wooton as a pastor
in 1880. John Henry Douglas and Iowa Yearly Meeting would make a
great team to develop the pastoral movement as he became the yearly
meeting's first General Superintendent in 1886. His "Superintendent's
Report" to the Iowa Yearly Meeting sessions of 1887 reveals some of
this development. At that time, Iowa Yearly Meeting was a large field

with meetings in Iowa, Wisconsin, Minnesota, Dakota Territory, Nebraska, Oregon, Washington Territory, California, and Texas. Overall, there were one hundred meetings with an average membership of one hundred each. "The need of pastors is quite generally admitted, and there are very few meetings in our yearly meeting that do not feel this need. The important question now is: suitable pastors and how to support them. These matters will require time for their adjustment."[9]

During his four years as General Superintendent, John Henry Douglas accomplished great changes as the pastoral system developed. In the conclusion of his last "Superintendent's Report" of 1890, some of these changes are made evident as he reflected upon his years in Iowa.

> It may be well for the Yearly Meeting to pause a few moments and take a good look at the results of the past four years of work under the present system. During that time our meetings have increased in number fifty per cent, over 2,500 added to the church by request. The number of ministers have increased from 138 to 180. The number of pastors have run up from three to seventy. Money raised to carry forward the work has increased about three hundred per cent.

> The number of those who have professed faith in Christ, more than eight thousand during the four years, and about forty new meeting houses have been built. The church is better united than ever before, more spiritual gifts are being exercised, and our schools are all stronger centers of spiritual life and activity.[10]

Strong concern about this new system of pastoral ministry came from London and from the East, particularly from the editorials and articles in the *Friends' Review*. Henry Hartshorne in the editorial of the *Review* on Jan. 27, 1887, recognized that other denominations may have good success with their pastoral systems, but that it did "not follow that their system was best."[11]

> Better, in other words, the full, practical recognition of the priesthood of all believers, and of the ordaining of ministers of the Gospel by the Head of the Church alone, than most wisely organized establishment, espiscopal, presbyterian, or any other.

> If this be so (and, if we do not believe it, we are not Friends), there is a duty of the Society to maintain the

standard given it to set up. No matter how good may be or
have been the work of others, this is our right position.
Abandonment of it is going backwards;—deformation
instead of reformation.[12]

In a private letter to Hartshorne, John Henry Douglas appealed to the
Review to cease its opposition of the system:

As one of those who receives help from the Church in
carrying out that which the Lord of the Church has laid
upon me, and representing *many* more *poor* ministers in like
situation enter my protest against the treatment we meet
with through the *Review*. . . Any hint that any of us are
preaching for money, or are dependent upon preaching to
make a living is utterly false. Or that we get in the way of
the development of others gifts *is not true*. Encouragement
seems to be given to every gift and its support except that
of a *poor* minister. If we were all rich these questions would
not arise. *Every one* rejoices to see men of *means devote
their whole* time to doing good. I enter my protest against a
paper meddling with *private* matters. Nearly all our
ministers in the Y.M. who receive assistance receive it
from their personal friends and no one is *taxed* for their
support.[13]

Hartshorne's response raised the whole question of church authority
and autonomy in the local monthly meetings and among the yearly
meetings.

How can I, after reading thy "protest," just received, but
enter a *counter-protest*,— against what I, as editor of
Friends' Review, never did nor thought of doing, being
charged upon me? Namely, *meddling* with *private* matters,
of ministers or others? For the question about a Yearly
Meeting, that of Iowa, has a discussion and adopts a
minute, and which concerns Monthly Meetings throughout
the Society of Friends everywhere, is *not* a private matter,
but a very important *public* one. It is twofold: 1. Shall it
be approved and recommended that, contrary to the usage of
the Society for two centuries, individual pastors shall be
placed in charge of individual congregations, instead of the
whole work of the Church being in charge of the *whole
church*, whether it has one, ten or no acknowledged
"ministers," or not; 2. Whether it is or is not to be
recommended that "ministers" shall, as has never before

this generation been the case among Friends, avoid secular business, and, when not possessed of means, expect to be supported *as* pastors or evangelists, by stated stipends or salaries? . . .

I honestly believe that a large amount of *harm* has already been done, *the whole unhealthy fruit of which has not yet been seen*, by those who have publicly advised and exhorted that young men in the Society of Friends should, when they think they are to be ministers, avoid secular engagements and throw themselves wholly into the ministry as their only avocation for life.[14]

New York Yearly Meeting also officially approved the pastoral system in 1886, the same year as Iowa. Due to the influence of *The Christian Worker*, which passed the details of ministry from yearly meeting to yearly meeting so well, other yearly meetings were liberated to take the step of this radical change. The yearly meetings of Kansas, Western, Ohio, and Indiana also began development of the pastoral system that same year, just prior to the Richmond Conference. Full approval was just around the corner!

The
Curtain Rises

The Conference Is Called

As the concerns in regard to the great diversity among Quakers mounted in the 1880s, the attention needs to be directed toward Timothy Nicholson of Indiana Yearly Meeting. After Ohio Yearly Meeting chose not to approve the affirmation of the Quaker traditional view on water baptism during its Yearly Meeting sessions of 1885, *The Christian Worker*, through the editorial work of Calvin Pritchard, became a tolerant mouthpiece of this change. After Indiana Yearly Meeting adopted a minute in its 1885 yearly meeting sessions reaffirming the Quaker historical position on the ordinances, Nicholson defended this action to the editor of the *Worker*. Nicholson wrote to Pritchard:

> I have found no one within the limits of our Yearly Meeting nor any other Yearly Meeting outside of Ohio who has objections to the prompt and decisive action of our Yearly Meeting—personal esteem—amounting almost to *man's worship* for D. B. Updegraff to outweigh all other considerations. Now our course was not occasioned by D. B. U.'s actions of departure, and not within our limits. So long as he and his followers continued their operations to their own units—we were quiet; but when they (his followers) invaded our territory, it was clearly our duty to act promptly and effectually.[1]

Due to the *Worker's* support of Updegraff, Nicholson took a strong stand against the journal. Since the *Worker* was the primary organ of western Friends, Nicholson and eleven other Friends of Western and Indiana Yearly Meetings joined together to publish the *Morning Star*, in Indianapolis, primarily to battle the *Worker's* position on baptism. "This exerted sufficient influence to change the policy and attitude of the *Christian Worker*."[2] Once this was accomplished the paper was discontinued.

But Nicholson did not stop his actions which expressed his deep concern for the Society. He, more than any other single person, provided the spark which would result in the Richmond Conference of 1887. His own story about this is as follows:

> During Indiana Yearly Meeting in 1886, I invited, of the ministers attending the Yearly Meeting, one from each of five other Yearly Meetings and Francis W. Thomas of our own, to take supper at our house one evening; and at the table I introduced the subject of a General Conference of the Yearly Meetings. I briefly advocated and expressed the conviction that this was the time for Indiana Yearly Meeting to take the lead in the matter. Barnabas Hobbs of Western Yearly Meeting, which under his leadership had twice proposed such a conference, ably supported what I had said; all the others agreed and we requested Francis W. Thomas to introduce the subject the next day to the Meeting.[3]

The next day during the 1886 annual sessions of Indiana Friends, Thomas brought the concern to the attention of the business meeting. A committee of thirty members was appointed to consider such a gathering. Members of this large committee included Timothy Nicholson, Allen Jay, Dougan Clark, Esther Frame, and Francis Thomas. This committee recommended in favor of such a conference and proposed the following minute for approval. This minute became an invitation which was appended to the epistles for corresponding yearly meetings.

> To Indiana Yearly Meeting:
>
> We, the committee appointed to consider the subject of a conference of the Yearly Meetings in America with which we correspond, are (with one exception) united in proposing that the following minute be adopted by the Yearly

Meeting, and that suitable steps be taken to lay the subject before the other Yearly Meetings for their consideration. And we nominate for delegates to the conference the Friends therein named:

MINUTE

The subject of a conference of committees from the different Yearly Meetings in America with which we correspond, having been introduced into this Meeting, after deliberate consideration it was believed that the holding of such a conference, to consider matters appertaining to the welfare of our branch of the church, would strengthen the bonds of Christian fellowship amongst us, and tend to promote unity in important matters of faith and practice, in the different bodies into which Friends in America are divided. We are therefore united in proposing to our sister Yearly Meetings in America, that such a conference be held, and that it be composed of delegates appointed by the different Yearly Meetings, its conclusions to be only advisory; but that at least five Yearly Meetings must unite in it, or the conference not be held.

We also propose that said conference be held next year (1887) in Richmond, Indiana, beginning on sixth-day following the close of Western Yearly Meeting, at 9 A.M., and we appoint as our delegates to the same: Francis W. Thomas, William P. Pinkham, Timothy Nicholson, Allen Jay, Thomas N. White, R.W. Douglas, Mahalah Jay, Naomi W. Harrison, Tamar T. Hill, Mary A. Goddard, Esther G. Frame, and Alice Bergman.

And we further propose that a cordial invitation be extended to London and Dublin Yearly Meetings to send delegates to this conference.

On behalf of the committee,
Mahalah Jay, Clerk of Committee[4]

The responses from the invited yearly meetings were extremely favorable. New England, New York, Baltimore, North Carolina, Ohio, Western, Iowa, Canada, and Kansas all joined with Indiana to represent all of the Orthodox American Yearly Meetings, except Philadelphia, which was not yet corresponding with the other yearly meetings. London and Dublin also responded in the affirmative to send representatives to the conference.

The concern was shared among the delegates of Indiana that Philadelphia should, at least, be "unofficially" represented at the conference. Early in 1887 Timothy Nicholson wrote James E. Rhoads expressing this concern:

> I think there will be a very general desire by the delegates to the proposed Conference at Richmond next ninth month, that Philadelphia Friends may be represented. We did not include Philadelphia Yearly Meeting in the proposition as we did not suppose any communication from our Yearly Meeting would ever be *read* in your Yearly Meeting. So far as I have conferred with the delegates of our own and Baltimore and Kansas Yearly Meetings, they all want a representation of Philadelphia Friends.[5]

After James Rhoads sent this letter to Henry Hartshorne, Hartshorne returned the letter with the attached note:

> As to the *manner* and *authority* of an invitation to Philadelphia delegates,—might it not come best from the *Representative Meeting* of Indiana Yearly Meeting?
>
> H. H.[6]

So on July 7, 1887, Nicholson sent the following invitation to James Rhoads, Henry Hartshorne, John Garrett, and David Scull:

> As we expected there seems to be a general desire by the delegates who have already been appointed to attend the proposed Conference of Friends...that some members of Philadelphia Yearly Meeting should also attend and at least participate in the deliberation and discussion of the subjects which may be considered by the Conference.
>
> As Indiana Yearly Meeting originated the proposition for the Conference, and as no session of our representative meeting will occur previous to the time named for the Conference, it seems fitting that its delegates should extend such an invitation as we can conventionally, not doubting, that the Conference when it meets will approve and endorse our action in this matter.
>
> A majority of the delegates appointed by Indiana Yearly Meeting have conferred to-gether, and they cordially unite in informing you that we desire your presence and counsel.[7]

When discovered, reaction to this invitation was swift and strong by David Updegraff. In the third issue of his new quarterly journal *Friends' Expositor* (July 1887), Updegraff wrote on "The Coming Conference." He had just read in *The London Friend* that J.B. Braithwaite reported to London Yearly Meeting that Philadelphia had made no appointment, but "a few Friends would go from thence to the conference by invitation in a non-official character."[8]

Updegraff responded:

> By whose invitation? Who are the Friends? How many of them? Who has *authority* to "invite?" If there are to be some "non-officials" why not more? Where is the provision for any? Such questions are to be asked on every side and they *will* be asked. And if brethren are really honest in this professed effort to "promote unity in America," they ought to be wise enough not to throw away their opportunity by flagrant disregard of the terms of the Conference, at least so long in advance of its meeting.[9]

Updegraff's contention was that a few "leading Friends" were determining such matters very quietly and that such undermining would "produce disruption instead of unity."[10] He continued in his editorial:

> There are too many members of the society that like straight forwardness and fair dealing, and that want to see a Conference of Quakers, where every member of it may at least have a possible chance for the immediate quidance of the Holy Spirit.[11]

William Nicholson sought to strengthen brother Timothy's invitation to the Philadelphia Quakers:

> For myself I gladly say that I should esteem it a great favor to meet all of you on that occasion. We have already been advised in certain quarters that your attendance at the Conference will meet with some opposition and I can readily appreciate any feeling of hesitation on your part because of this.[12]

Other Friends also had their attention fixed on the upcoming Conference. Joseph Walton, editor of *The Friend*, Philadelphia's

Conservative Quaker publication, cautioned Quakers about the problems that conferences can produce. He reminded his readers of the conferencing of 1849, 1851, and 1853, and the disunity which resulted from heavy-handed ultimatums issued through the directives of the conference.[13]

It is interesting to note the diversity of views in regard to the function and authority of the conference.

Updegraff wrote that the conference's powers are not legislative, but "advisory" only.

English Friends were also concerned about the authority of the conference. About one month prior to the conference, Henry Hartshorne sought to diminish London's fears in this regard when he wrote to J.S. Sewell, an English Quaker.

> I think the idea of a *tribunal* is hardly favored by any; only advisory not legislative duty and power being given to the Conference. But just now it may be not easy for English Friends to realize how serious the crisis with us is and what need for positive declarations on some subjects was created by the revolutionary course of extreme leaders, such as D.B. Updegraff and a few others.[14]

On the other hand, some Friends were placing a great hope in the conference to be the restoration of the Society. W. L. Pearson of Iowa Yearly Meeting knew that "revolutionary" leaders would be at the conference and wrote Timothy Nicholson just days before the conference.

> Several of the Ohio delegation will be Updegraffites, as from one to three from Iowa, and we may expect one or two from Western, I trust not more. But there will be no difficulty in pronouncing against ordinances. I have greater fears in regard to doctrine, and still greater that matters of church policy and organization may be lightly passed by or else too much done...

> I also sincerely hope that a biennial or, perhaps better, a triennial Conference of American Yearly Meetings may be decided upon at this Conference. It is much needed and it will be much easier to do it now than when grave questions have arisen in the future to call a Conference to settle them.[15]

But the strongest call for central organization for Friends with authority came from William Nicholson. As early as 1880 he articulated his definite conviction on such a topic in a series of articles in the *Friends' Review* entitled "Serious Thoughts for Serious Friends." Three months prior to the conference he wrote a lengthy letter compiling such thoughts once again:

> I have been persuaded for perhaps a score of years, that the weak point in the present organization of the Society of Friends is the independence of the Yearly Meetings, or in other words, the lack of a Central Body of ultimate authority and appeal in matters of Doctrine, Discipline and Practice...To my mind this has always been a fatal defect...

> Of course we cannot by any method remedy the *past*—we cannot even remedy the *present* perfectly. A Conference or Assembly with plenary powers cannot take hold of *present issues* and settle them without more or less of a crash. But the adoption of such a measure now may prevent much future trouble and add greatly to the vitality of the Church.

> A Central Body, with a proper Constitution, but supreme under that Constitution, would provide a Declaration of Faith—and a Scheme of Discipline and Practice for all matters...and would also provide for the publication of *one* central organ of the Society, to be the property of the Church...instead of a half dozen periodicals which now tend to divide rather than edify.

> I do not know that the views above expressed are shared by a single individual who will be in the Conference. I do not know but even my dear brother Timothy will think that I have lost my head. Well, I have given much thought to this subject for a long time and especially of late, feeling the responsibility of the service laid upon me and my fellow delegates, and being assured that constant disintegration must ultimate in the ruin of our beloved Society. I am ready to adopt the only measure which seems to me at all adequate to the imperative needs of the time.[16]

And in a letter written to his brother just three days before the opening of the Conference, William Nicholson penned these words:

> Our Yearly Meetings are too much like mass meetings— easily swayed by zeal, earnestness, enthusiasm, declaration,

and impassioned delivery. We need a *deliberative* body for the settlement of great questions. It is *the* question of the hour. Temporizing will no longer do. We must have something permanent.[17]

The Conference: The First Four Considerations

In accordance with the Minutes of Indiana Yearly Meeting of last year, a conference of the Society of Friends, composed of delegates appointed by all the Yearly Meetings in the world, except that of Philadelphia, convened in Richmond, Ind., in Friends' Eighth Street Meeting House, on Sixth-day, Ninth mo. 23rd, 1887, near the hour of 9 o'clock in the forenoon.[1]

The following account of the opening meeting and seating of the delegates was taken from *The Interchange* (Baltimore). It was recorded in the *Proceedings* since there was not a stenographer's record of the first two sessions.

The 23rd of Ninth Month was a bright and beautiful morning in Richmond, Indiana, and all the delegates from all the Yearly Meetings in the world came together in the Eighth Street Friends' Meeting-house, their greetings of one another were warm and hearty. Some had met many times before, some had never seen each other, but all seemed to recognize at once the fact, that they were one family with a common bond and common interest. . .

The Conference was opened by J. Bevan Braithwaite, of London, who spoke beautifully and briefly. He said that this was the first Conference ever held composed of delegates from all the Yearly Meetings, and that it was a most important and significant gathering, and that it was fitting that we should begin our deliberations with a time of solemn waiting on the Lord and prayer. . .

Timothy Nicholson, on the part of the Indiana delegation, said that, as it had been suggested that they should arrange for the first session, to save time, he should name Francis W. Thomas as Chairman for the day, and Dr. William Nicholson and Mahalah Jay as Secretaries. Francis W. Thomas made a few opening remarks, and read some verses from the Bible. J. Bevan Braithwaite followed in prayer, and for more than an hour prayers were offered in succession. All asked in beautiful unity that the Lord's will might be done in us and through us, that we might be bound together in His love, have the power of the Holy Ghost resting upon us, and be made effective for our Lord and Savior in the world. It was worth the whole journey to Richmond just for this opportunity, for it brought us so near together in the love and power of God. . .

The question in regard to the admission of the Friends from Philadelphia Yearly Meeting claimed attention. . . . It was considered to be an exceptional case. J.B. Braithwaite said he hoped all understood the peculiar position of Philadelphia Yearly Meeting. He trusted that we would not only admit them, but give them a cordial welcome. Allen Jay endorsed these remarks, and said he hoped they would be given "here and now a cordial welcome." All at once there was an expression of approval all over the Conference and the Chairman also extended a welcome to them in the name of the Conference.[2]

Minutes and representatives from twelve yearly meetings were recognized. A total of ninety-five delegates were in attendance at this major gathering of Orthodox, Gurneyite Quakers. Many weighty Friends, the movers and shakers in the Society, were in attendance and gave leadership throughout the conference. Some of those weighty Friends were representatives, as follows: Joseph Bevan Braithwaite and George Gillett, London; George Grubb, Dublin; James Wood, New York; James Cary Thomas and Mary W. Thomas, Baltimore; Joseph Moore, North Carolina; David B. Updegraff and Israel P. Hole, Ohio; Timothy Nicholson, Allen Jay, Mahalah Jay, Esther Frame and Robert W. Douglas, Indiana; Barnabas Hobbs and Calvin Pritchard, Western;

Benjamin Trueblood and John Henry Douglas, Iowa; and William Nicholson, Kansas.

The weighty Friends from Philadelphia whom the conference welcomed were James Rhoads, Henry Hartshorne, David Scull, and John Garrett. They were invited to participate in the discussions but not to serve on committees nor to have a voice in the decisions of the conference. A note was also made in the early minutes that "our aged Friend, Eli Jones, of New England Yearly Meeting, was invited to a seat on the floor of the conference."[3]

A Committee on Permanent Organization was appointed. A Business Committee was appointed to consider and formulate the propositions to be presented for the deliberation of the Conference. A request was granted for a stenographer to keep an accurate record of the proceedings of the Conference.

During the afternoon session, the Committee on Permanent Organization recommended James Wood of New York Yearly Meeting as Chairman, and Jehu Stuart of Iowa Yearly Meeting and Mahalah Jay of Indiana Yearly Meeting as Clerks.

The Business Committee proposed the following guidelines:

1. Three regular sessions of the Conference shall be held each day, on Sixth, Seventh, and Second-days. The opening session will begin at 9:00 a.m. and end at noon. The afternoon session will begin at 3:00 p.m. and end at 5:00 p.m. And the evening session will begin at 7:00 p.m. and end at 9:00 p.m.
2. Spouses of the delegates shall be admitted to the floor of the Conference, and each delegation shall have the privilege of inviting not more than ten persons as visitors to the sessions.
3. Ordinary methods in use among Friends would be observed in determining the decisions of the Conference.
4. Each delegate would be recognized by the Chairman, and the name of the speaker and his or her Yearly Meeting would be distinctly announced.
5. No speaker should occupy more than 20 minutes in one address without consent of the Chairman, and no speaker should speak a second time on any one proposition without consent of the Chairman. The second address should not exceed five minutes.
6. The committee recommended a stenographer for the Conference.

Eleven intense sessions over a total of five days would make up this conference from Friday, Sept. 23, until Tuesday, Sept. 27. No sessions were held on Sunday, Sept. 25. Three sessions were held each day at 9:00 a.m., 3:00 p.m., and 7:00 p.m., except for the last day when only afternoon and evening sessions were held.

Of the ninety-five delegates participating in the conference, sixty-one men and thirty-four women represented the twelve yearly meetings. Ohio had the largest representation with fourteen delegates. Indiana had twelve delegates with Iowa and Western each represented by eleven. New England, New York, and Baltimore each sent eight delegates. The rest of the numerical representation was as follows: London, six; Kansas, six; Canada, five; Dublin, three; and North Carolina, three. (And Philadelphia had the four unofficial delegates.)

A stenographer's record was kept beginning with the evening session on Friday, which was the conference's third session. This was the first session that actually began the discussion on the considerations before the conference.

To give a statistical flavor of how much each of the delegates contributed to the discussions, the following is a record taken from examining the *Proceedings*. Of the ninety-five delegates, twenty-five delegates did not speak at all; twelve of these were men and thirteen were women. Twenty-one delegates were recorded as speaking only once, and twelve of these were men while nine were women. Nineteen only spoke two or three times, and among these were ten men and nine women. This means that sixty-five of the ninety-five delegates spoke only three times or even less.

On the other hand, a small handful carried the bulk of the dialogue with only fourteen speaking at least ten different times, and this number includes James Wood, the Conference Chairman. These people, all men, should be recognized as the pacemakers of the discussions. They are Joseph Bevan Braithwaite and Joseph Storrs Fry, London; James Cary Thomas, Baltimore; David B. Updegraff and Israel P. Hole, Ohio; Timothy Nicholson, Allen Jay, and Robert W. Douglas, Indiana; Barnabas Hobbs and Calvin Pritchard, Western; and Isom P. Wooton, Benjamin Trueblood, and John Henry Douglas, Iowa. These thirteen weighty Friends spoke a total of 195 times throughout the conference. The other eighty-one delegates spoke only a total of 163 different times during the conference.

Of course, talking a great deal or speaking on several occasions didn't necessarily mean that was the only way one was a "weighty" Friend. The Philadelphia delegates did not speak much, but their opinions seem to be held in high esteem, especially the words of James Rhoads and Henry Hartshorne who spoke only six and seven times, respectively.

However, those messages were usually lengthy addresses. Also, George Gillett (London), George Grubb (Dublin), Mary W. Thomas and Mary S. Thomas (Balt.), Francis Thomas and Esther Frame (Ind.), Charles Hutchison (Iowa), and William Nicholson (Kansas) spoke powerfully, yet not as often as the others.

Even though the conference was not highly organized, some committees were appointed throughout the conference. The following four committees reveal leadership and representation:

Committee on Permanent Organization

Joseph Storrs Fry (Lon.), Thomas White Fisher (Dub.), William D. Newhall (N.E.), William H.S. Wood (N.Y.), Caleb Winslow (Balt.), Abigail Mendenhall (N.C.), John Butler (Ohio), Allen Jay (Ind.), Nathan Clark (West.), Isom P. Wooton (Iowa), William Coffin (Kan.), and John Dorland (Can.)[4]

Business Committee

Charles Brady (Lon.), George Grubb (Dub.), Augustine Jones (N.E.), Augustus Taber (N.Y.), James Cary Thomas (Balt.), Joseph Moore (N.C.), Jacob Baker (Ohio), Timothy Nicholson (Ind.), David Hadley (West.), Benjamin Trueblood (Iowa), William Nicholson (Kan.), and Howard Nicholson (Can.)[5]

Subcommittee to Receive Subjects for Consideration

Charles Brady, David Hadley, Augustus Taber, Timothy Nicholson, and Benjamin Trueblood[6]

Committee to Prepare Conclusions

Joseph Storrs Fry (Lon.), Ruth S. Murray (N.E.), Francis Thomas (Ind.), William Nicholson (Kan.), and Isom P. Wooton (Iowa)[7]

Committee to Prepare a Declaration of Faith

Joseph Bevan Braithwaite (Lon.), William Nicholson (Kan.), George Grubb (Dub.), James Cary Thomas (Balt.), James Wood (N.Y.), Joseph Moore (N.C.), Barnabas Hobbs (West.), Jane White (Balt.), Benjamin Trueblood (Iowa), George Gillett (Lon.), Jacob Baker (Ohio), and Mahalah Jay (Ind.)[8]

The conference centered around the discussion of six specific questions or topics. *The Proceedings of Friends' Conference 1887* recorded them in the following ways.

1. Is it desirable that all the Yearly Meetings of Friends in the world should adopt one declaration of Christian doctrine?
2. What is the mission of the Society of Friends; what is its message to the world; and how can we best fulfill and declare them?
3. Is it desirable that there should be a union of the American Yearly Meetings in foreign mission work?
4. Discussion on the subject of the ordinances.
5. Meetings for worship, and the method of conducting them.
6. What is the relation of the ministry to the church, and the church to the ministry, and how shall the ministry be sustained?[9]

The Friday evening session opened with the first question from the Business Committee: "Is it desirable that all the Yearly Meetings of Friends in the world should adopt one declaration of Christian doctrine?"

Francis Thomas (Ind.) opened the discussion and the concerns in regard to the question. First, he expressed concern about "creeds" and recognized the "Sacred Volume" as the only creed for Friends. However, the enlightenment of the Holy Spirit to understand the scriptures must always be held as the testimony of Friends. Therefore, the message of Friends would be distinquished from other religious bodies. Secondly, he recognized the divergence even within Friends, from yearly meeting to yearly meeting. The conference could unite Friends for the future if they would pause now and re-emphasize "the basis of unity and oneness in the common faith." Third, he suggested that a "special committee" be appointed for the formulation of such a declaration.

James Rhoads (Phil.) was the next delegate to speak. His lengthy speech (25-30 minutes because he went overtime) affirmed the writing of such a declaration, and he cited the great issues of Christian doctrine—God, Jesus Christ, the Holy Spirit, the scriptures, Universal Light, atonement, the Church, justification, sanctification, peace, oaths, etc. However, in this lengthy presentation, he did not even mention the ordinances. Yet he set the pace and outlined an understanding of what this declaration might look like.

Rhoads was followed by lengthy remarks from Israel P. Hole (Ohio), Mary W. Thomas (Balt.), Charles Brady (Lon.), Jacob Baker (Ohio),

James Cary Thomas (Balt.), Timothy Nicholson (Ind.), Barnabas Hobbs (West.), David B. Updegraff (Ohio), and Henry Hartshorne (Phil.). All of them argued in the affirmative except for Updegraff.

Mary W. Thomas raised the additional issues of baptism and communion, ministry, and, particularly, women. She revealed great insight in considering the name for such a declaration:

> I would like the question better if it were stated as a declaration of Christian faith, rather than Christian doctrine. It seems to me that that is what the church is called to do, to express its faith in God, its faith in the Lord Jesus Christ, and its faith in the Holy Ghost. I believe that all the testimonies of early Friends were in this direction. They were affirmative. It was not so much statement of doctrine with them, as I have said, as a statement of faith.[10]

Charles Brady affirmed the question by stating that Friends need not fear the word sectarianism. He said that "it is God's purpose, in the present time at least, to work largely through the divisions of the Christian Church."[11]

Jacob Baker reminded the delegates that not all the major points of Christian doctrine had yet been mentioned in the discussion, namely resurrection and eternal judgment.

The words of James Carey Thomas powerfully spoke to the concerns of having a creed:

> When a creed has been agreed upon and formulated, the orthodoxy of a member has often been tested, not by the Scripture, but by the creed. This is one thing that has made an objection to a creed. What we want is a creed so formulated on the Scripture as the light of Scripture is thrown upon it, that we might have a common expression of our faith; and I believe this period in history of Friends is one peculiarly fitted for that. There are those among us who might pass away if a long period was allowed to elapse, whose judgment, experience, and Christian insight would be valuable to us at this particular stage of our experience as a church.[12]

Barnabas Hobbs also answered the question affirmatively primarily because the Friends understanding of the Christian faith could not be found in any one book or place. Barclay's *Apology* was used to compare Friends to other churches of that day. Evans' *Exposition* could distinquish the differences between the Orthodox and the Hicksite. And William Penn only wrote about subjects where the Anglican Church and the Quakers disagreed.

David Updegraff related three points in opposition to the question. First, he reminded the delegates that often the Holy Spirit gave early Friends new language, other than the Biblical words, to convey the Gospel messages. Perhaps Friends at the conference needed to discard the old language of the earlier Quakers as well. Secondly, Updegraff felt that the current *Disciplines* of the various yearly meetings were entirely sufficient, even though there were some "slight discrepancies, or distinctions, according to the attitude of the different Yearly Meetings."[13] There was also a "substantial agreement in all of these declarations."[14] Third, Updegraff referred to the current edition of *The London Friend* and agreed with its editor's remarks on the upcoming conference:

> If questions of doctrine are to be settled, it will be an evil day for the Society when it swerves from its ancient practice of owning no creed but the Scripture. If questions of church discipline need consideration, it seems to us that grave difficulties will arise, if any attempt be made to interfere with the independent action of individual Yearly Meetings.[15]

This first question was finally returned to the Business Committee without any action by the conference. If the way would open again, it would be taken up at a future session of the conference.

The next morning, Saturday, the fourth session engaged the second question from the Business Committee: "What is the mission of the Society of Friends, and what is its message to the world, and how can we best fulfill and declare them?" This general question allowed the delegates to again open the issues of concern for Friends. Joseph B. Braithwaite, Francis Thomas, James Cary Thomas, Benjamin Trueblood, Barnabas Hobbs, Esther Frame, George Gillett, John Dorland, and Israel P. Hole all gave lengthy dissertations on the topic covering a wide variety of thought. The most significant item of discussion was the subject of women. Apparently referring to a comment made outside of the conference deliberations, Esther Frame placed this issue squarely in front of the conference.

> John Henry Douglas said we do not want the woman question raised, but we do want the woman question, and

there is no doubt that in this we need more saving, real, personal salvation, being born of the Spirit, washed, sanctified, filled with the Holy Ghost, and walking with God; there is not any one subject that we need to leave before the world more than the privileges the Gospel brings to womankind, and I feel the importance of our maintaining that principle of making no difference between man and woman. We scarcely realize this necessity until we go out into the world and see how women are held in bondage. As I have been in the South land, I have seen many women, qualified and refined, who might be a power in the world, and as I looked into those congregations last summer, into their bright, intelligent faces, I thought very much as I did when I stood by the Niagara Falls. I said, "What a waste of power!" And so I uphold the standard of woman. Women must work. . . . I do not think we have any testimony to lower in the least, but I believe that we ought to hoist them still higher in the breeze. . . .[16]

At the end of the session, John Henry Douglas did defend the earlier statement which he was quoted as saying in regard to women.

What I stated in relation to the woman question I want to go on record just as I stated it. In a Friends' meeting, the question is settled. It is settled in Friends' testimony, in our books and our history, that in Christ there is neither male nor female; we are one in Christ. We make no reference whatever in our worship, preaching, appointing committees, or whatever it is, to sex, the suitability of the occasion and the leading of the Spirit, as I understand it, being followed in this work.[17]

However, the question of women was sufficiently brought to the light, and it would be discussed further in the future sessions.

This second question would find the greatest unanimity among the delegates during the conference. The "Conclusions" speak of living the truth which has always marked the distinctiveness of the testimonies.

. . .whilst in common with our fellow-Christians we have to proclaim the fundamental truths of the Gospel, fully accepting the historical record of all that our Savior did and suffered; his birth, his teachings, his holy life, his death for the sins of the world, his resurrection and ascension; we have to testify to the practical realization of these truths in our own experience, and to the duty of carrying out in our

daily life all that belongs to their spiritual application. . . .
These truths are needed by the world, and should be carried
into all the reforms of the day, as an energizing, purifying
influence, which shall tend to the glory of God, and the
blessing of the world.[18]

The Saturday afternoon session dealt with the question: "Is it
desirable that there should be a union of the yearly meetings for foreign
mission work?"

Mahalah Jay gave some background to this question stating that
most of the yearly meetings are doing work individually with the
cooperation of other yearly meetings.

I believe that one or two Yearly Meetings have no separate
work of their own, but contribute in money or other ways,
perhaps through some committee, to another Yearly
Meeting's work. But as our work stands now, we are so
many different missionary organizations not working
together and not working against each other. We are simply
separated and isolated in our work.[19]

The consensus in the following discussion was an affirmative answer
to the question, and as the "Conclusions" stated: "It is desirable to have
one central board of missions, whose actions would unify the efforts
now put forth by the different yearly meetings, and enable them to work
more wisely and efficiently."[20]

Once again, however, the subject turned to the role of women,
because the mission work was being supported by the Women's
Foreign Missionary Societies in many of the yearly meetings. In
Canada Yearly Meeting the men had turned the foreign mission work
completely over to the women.   And most other yearly meetings at
least had the work "greatly stimulated by our sisters in their
organizations."[21]

Eliza C. Armstrong (West.) challenged the women: "Sisters, I want
to appeal to you; let us rally at this time, and God grant we may be the
Deborah to drive into captivity this spirit of separateness that has been
the bane of the Yearly Meetings on this continent."[22]

But Mary W. Thomas gave the most stirring address on this topic of
missions, but even more so on the topic of women:

I would be very sorry to see the women of the Society of
Friends take the position of those in the Methodist church

as auxiliary to any board of men. The women in the Society of Friends hold a different position from that held by them in any other church. Our place is side by side with our brethren. . . Now we have talked here about the success of this work and the women doing this work, and the men have disapproved of it; but it is time that the men in the Society of Friends should remember the place of the women in it, and they will hear this question brought up again and again and again. The women in the Society of Friends have a position that is not allowed them by their brethren nor given to them by man. It is given to them by the Head of the church, the Lord Jesus Christ. There is neither male nor female in Christ Jesus. This Society is the only society that professes that woman should have this place, and it is organized on that basis, and we are not going to let you forget it, and it will come up continually, and I do say that the men of the Society of Friends need to be reminded of it.[23]

In regard to several delegates' concerns for the consideration of the ordinances, the Business Committee brought the following report to the Saturday evening (sixth) session of the conference as a resolution to this third concern:

TO THE CONFERENCE: A number of suggestions having been made by members of the Conference to the Business Committee, in reference to the teaching and practice of Water Baptism and the Supper, by those in official positions in the Society of Friends, the committee have given careful attention thereto, but believe that the recent official utterances and reaffirmations of eight Yearly Meetings on this continent have definitely settled these questions. They present with this report an extract from the Minutes of Indiana Yearly Meeting, which is in substantial agreement with the minutes of other Yearly Meetings; and we advise that the subject be not entered upon or debated at this time. The extract from the Minute of Indiana Yearly Meeting is as follows: "We believe it to be inconsistent for any one to be acknowledged or retained in the position of Minister or Elder among us who continues to participate in or to teach the necessity of the outward rite of Baptism or the Supper."[24]

Benjamin Trueblood pointed out on behalf of the Business Committee that it was not the intention of the committee that the

Indiana Yearly Meeting Minute should be adopted or rejected. It was merely a part of the report as a sample of previous yearly meetings' actions.

With very, very brief discussion and with David B. Updegraff giving a final comment, the report was "adopted as the sentiment of the body."[25]

Updegraff's comment needs to be examined.

> I desire to express my hearty acquiescence in the report of the committee as the very best thing, and the very least thing, doubtless, that this Conference could be expected to do. I appreciate, I think, very highly indeed, the spirit of brotherly love and condescension and desire upon the part of the committee to say something to which none of us would object. I desire to say that much.[26]

The Conference:
The Last Two Considerations

With the decision not to debate the ordinances (supposedly finished in terms of the conference), the Saturday evening session went on to the discussion of "public meetings for worship, and the manner of conducting them," which constituted the fifth topic of consideration. The Business Committee particularly meant the "regularly established meetings for worship" in regard to the "public meetings for worship."

This subject entertained a discussion in which the differences among the gathered delegates became more apparent. George Grubb (Dub.) opened the discussion by building a strong defense for the "common ground of silent waiting upon the Lord."[1] Silent worship provides the basis for the spiritual union of the believer with Jesus Christ, for a gathered meeting to be held in the power of the Lord, and for the two or three gathered in His name to hear what His will is. The two areas of worship which needed caution, according to Grubb, were congregational singing and hymn singing.

> If we for one moment adopt the practice of congregational singing from books, we may just as reasonably adopt the practice of praying from books. . . . And I hope that we may keep the position that we do not want to admit any books into our congregational worship except that one Book, the Holy Scriptures of Truth.[2]

Grubb's major concern against the bringing in of written prayers and hymns was that there could be disunity nurtured in regard to the authority of such writings.

Next, Joseph B. Braithwaite spoke at length. His comments were quite general except his emphasis that "the immediate, direct teaching of the Spirit of God. . . is not dependent upon outward ordinances or upon the presence of of an outward minister."[3]

The discussion followed with many Friends on the western frontier giving a rebuttal to the subtle "eldering" from the Friends across Atlantic and the eastern Friends. Friends from the Midwest spoke of the need of clear preaching to convict sinners, thorough teaching to equip new converts, and edification through the spoken word to challenge all believers.

Such diversity could be discovered in many comments during the discussion. Jane Votaw (Iowa) said: "I have been in silent meetings. I was raised in a silent meeting. I was raised in a meeting where they sat silent for an hour, and I do not remember of ever seeing one soul brought into the fold of Christ."[4]

On the other hand, Joseph Storrs Fry sought to counter some of this discussion: "I do not feel for myself that singing is wrong. . . But it does not appear to me that it would, as a general rule, add to the edification or very greatly help our ordinary meetings for worship."[5]

Perhaps the discussion of this subject gave the delegates a greater understanding, and even appreciation, for the growing differences of practice in regard to worship. One of the obvious differences seemed to be that the spiritual needs of an established meeting of the East, London, or Dublin did vary from the spiritual needs of a newly established meeting. Still, it was affirmed that the guidance of the Head of the Church should always be sought in silent waiting in all meetings, but that the ministry of the word, prayer, and the reading of the scriptures would be beneficial for the exaltation of Christ and the blessing of those gathered. Caution was given about undue activity which might prevent the hearing of the still, small voice of the Spirit. Singing especially could be a distraction to spiritual worship if it wasn't suited to the particular conditions of those present or if it appeared to be more entertainment than worship.

The conference resumed on Monday morning at 9:00 a.m. After the record of the sessions on Saturday was read, a lengthy and technical discussion ensued in regard to the earlier report on the subject of the ordinances from Saturday evening. It was decided that the subject should be returned to the Business Committee to reword its resolution according to the very divergent sentiments of the conference. It was thought that, especially, the reference to the Indiana Yearly Meeting should be removed.

Next, the Business Committee presented the following recommendation:

> The Conference having decided that one declaration of Christian doctrine is desirable, we recommend that a committee be appointed to prepare from the established Disciplines and declarations of faith of the different Yearly Meetings a restatement of our Christian beliefs as a religious Society, and report to a future session of this Conference.[6]

After another technical discussion, the proposition was changed and approved as follows:

> The Conference having decided that one Declaration of Christian Doctrine is desirable, we therefore recommend that a committee be appointed to prepare a statement of our Christian belief, as a branch of the Church of Christ, and report to a future session of the Conference.[7]

The committee to prepare the document was also nominated by the Business Committee. With one change, this committee's members were J. B. Braithwaite, William Nicholson, George Grubb, James C. Thomas, James Wood, Joseph Moore, Barnabas Hobbs, Mary W. Thomas, Benjamin Trueblood, George Gillett, Jacob Baker, and Mahalah Jay. Each yearly meeting had one delegate represented on this committee except for Canada and New England, which were not represented, and London and Baltimore, which had two delegates.

After approval of these names, Calvin Pritchard (West.) suggested "an additional name. . .that I think would give relief to some of the friends of this Conference."[8]

James Wood, the Chairman, responded that that would "open a very dangerous door. . . . it is not fair to entertain a proposition of that kind."[9]

It is extremely interesting to note that the Declaration was already in the process of being written, as the three following personal accounts show.

Joseph Bevan Braithwaite:

I am always anxious to be perfectly open, and I feel that there is nothing to conceal; much as I desire that particular individuals should be mixed up with the authorship of public documents as little as possible. I specially avoided taking any part in the deliberation as to the expediency of a Declaration. The responsibility felt to me so great. When it was concluded upon, Dr. Jas. C. Thomas and, I think, another friend asked me about it. I told them that I felt it a very serious thing to enter upon, and supposed that it was so left. This was on 6th day evening. Then on 7th day either in the morning or after Dr. Thomas spoke to me again with great urgency, saying that it was very important that something should be done. I at last told him that I felt it a very solemn thing, and could not venture to *undertake* to do anything; but that if they could arrange for Dr. Rhoads to assist me, he and I would, in great fear and very prayerfully, yield ourselves to make the attempt, on the understanding that it was to be a simple compilation from accredited documents, principally our Book of Discipline, etc. So it was left for him to arrange with Dr. Rhoads. On First day morning I went quietly with our dear friend John Butler to New Garden, about 10 miles from Richmond, returning in the afternoon. On reaching my quarters at Allen Jay's private study, I found that Dr. Rhoads was ready to join me. We entered upon the work from paragraph to paragraph. Dr. Rhoads kindly wrote to my dictation and proved a most, sweet, loving, tender and efficient helper. There was no hurry or bustle, but all proceeded in absolute retirement in Allen Jay's private study and in great sweetness of spirit. We worked at it without interruption, except meals and needful rest from about 7:00 p.m. on First day to noon on Third day, rising early and sitting late, and throughout with such precious intervals of worship and prayer. *Nothing was prepared beforehand*—not a word was put upon paper before we began as stated on First day evening. Neither Dr. Rhoads nor I attended any of the sittings of the Conference on Second day, or 3rd day morning; and I was not present when the committee was appointed and only heard of it from Allen Jay on his return to dinner. The idea that we any of us took anything ready prepared from England is entirely without foundation. The above is the simple statement of what actually occurred. Being compilation, the materials were in our book of Discipline, the New York Discipline, the Discipline issued by the Lancashire Committee and perhaps one ot two other documents.

The whole was carefully twice read and considered *very deliberately* by the committee of the 12 at Allen Jay's house on 3rd day morning. It was generally approved; but some valuable suggestions were made. About half of it was brought to the afternoon sitting of the Conference—and the remainder in the evening. The labour of Dr. Rhoads and myself was simply tentative, and we were quite prepared to have it set aside by the committee of 12. There was nothing like forcing—the matter was felt to be deeply important. Of course, I should have ben *very thankful* if more time could have been given to it in the Conference. All that we can say is, we endeavoured humbly and tremblingly to do our best.[10]

Timothy Nicholson:

Dr. James E. Rhoads, President of Bryn Mawr College, was amanuensis for the committee. Joseph B. Braithwaite (of London Yearly Meeting) was the distinquished leader. No other man could have accomplished the feat in the time allowed. He brought with him numerous books of Discipline containing Yearly Meeting declarations of faith, pamphlets on Friends' doctrines, and many of the issues of the London Yearly Meeting's General Epistle, which, for at least twenty years, he himself had drafted. From all this material his marvelous legal ability evolved or compiled this unique Declaration of Faith. No entirely new matter was introduced, but it was the grouping together of what had already passed London and other Yearly Meetings from time to time.

At three P.M. the last day a part of the document was presented to the Conference, read, discussed and approved, but much yet remained to be done. J.B. Braithwaite stopped at Allen Jay's, a mile distant, and there is where the committee met. The work must be completed by 7 P.M. and every minute was important. Our home was only a square from South Eighth Street Meetinghouse in which the Conference was held. James Wood asked me if it would be possible for dear Mary to provide supper for the committee of twelve and their clerk (it was then after four o'clock). I replied I would run over and find out. My dear good wife said, "Yes, we will be ready by a few minutes after six." The committee came before five. We placed a table in the front room for J.B. Braithwaite and Dr. Rhoads.

When supper was ready all but these two went to the table. After the others had eaten, Mary and James Wood, at the latter's suggestion, took some tea and crackers and quietly set them on the table of the two workers and in a few minutes after seven the work was completed, taken to the Meetinghouse, read, discussed, and approved.[11]

Allen Jay:

A committee of twelve was appointed to draft the said declaration of faith. . . The committee met, and different ones were appointed to prepare certain sections of the declaration, but the greater portion of it was prepared by our late dear friend, Joseph Bevan Braithwaite, of London Yearly Meeting. It was written at the desk where I am now sitting. When he left home, thinking that something of the kind might claim the attention of the conference, he put in with his baggage several books and manuscripts that were prepared by the earlier writers among Friends and had not been changed by Friends of more recent date in this country or anywhere else. His remark was: "We want the original Quakerism free from the influence and thought of some of our Friends who have imbibed some of the spirit and practice of other denominations or have been influenced by their environments." Our dear friend worked early and late when not in the conference. I remember lying on the lounge until he quit writing near midnight, and then taking him to the dining room and getting him something to eat before he retired. Then in the morning he was up before anyone else. This was the case for two nights. Before it was presented to the conference it was gone over carefully, Joseph Bevan Braithwaite sitting at the desk reading carefully what had been written, Dr. James E. Rhoads, of Philadelphia, looking over the quotations from Friends writings to see that they were correct quoted, and Dr. James Cary Thomas, of Baltimore, watching the Scripture quotations to see that there were no mistakes made there. They have all three passed away, but their work remains. Next morning, after it was adopted by the conference, Joseph Bevan Braithwaite handed me the pen he wrote it with and said: "Thee may have that to keep." I have it yet.[12]

The last subject for discussion sent by the Business Committee was "the proper relation of the ministry to the Church and the duty of the Church toward the ministry, in connection with the liberty of prophesying and the necessity of maintaining it inviolate in all our meetings."

Isom P. Wooton (Iowa) moved to substitute the above consideration with the following question: "Would not some modification of our system of birthright membership be advisable?" But it was decided to begin discussion on the ministerial relationship to the church and to continue this subject into future sessions.

Charles Brady (Lon.) gave an explanation on behalf of the Business Committee about this subject of the ministry. A large number of questions came to the committee covering a broad spectrum of concern. Brady reviewed some of these questions and concerns to reveal the wide consideration of the subject.

> Is it consistent with the Headship of Christ in His Church, the priesthood of believers, or the freedom of the ministry of the Gospel, to employ a person as the salaried minister of a congregation? Another is: The unsuitableness of routine or prearranged exercises in religious meetings. Another is against the assumption of the term Reverend. And there are others, such as pastoral questions, the gift of the ministry, the gift of the teacher, and the pecuniary support of a pastor. All these are included in this question thrown open before us.[13]

These questions brought forth the longest discussion, and sometimes debate, that the conference experienced. More than eighty pages of the total 281 pages of discussion in the *Proceedings* dealt with this subject. The chairman had previously asked Thomas White Fisher of Dublin to open the consideration of these questions. He spoke in quite general terms but did a good job of opening the door of discussion in a somewhat objective way: "And may the Lord bless us every one, which ever side of the house we may be on, and help us to occupy our ministry faithfully to the praise and glory of Him who hath called us and given us the exalted positon of embassador of Christ."[14]

Calvin Pritchard (West.) was the first one to begin to build the case for the pastoral system.

> I feel like stating the situation of the church with relation to the ministry, as I understand its needs in this great Western country. There has ever been, and is now, a great demand for the ministry of the Word. Every minister, who is a man of much prominence, is sought for to go to various places where there are meetings of Friends, and

> where there are no ministers to preach the Gospel. The people want to hear—there is a great demand in this direction.[15]

Several other positive speeches were given in support of the pastoral system. John Henry Douglas was quite well prepared for this discussion. He came with written materials to explain the course of action in regard to the pastoral system that Iowa Yearly Meeting had been taking. He thoroughly presented Iowa's decisions and his reflections on the progress.

> In view of the criticisms that have been passed, I wanted you to know upon what basis we are acting. I am acting as general superintendent of the pastoral and evangelistic work in Iowa Yearly Meeting. This has been going on just one year, and the outcome has been perfectly surprising to ourselves, in the kindness with which our churches and our ministers received this, and the harmony and fellowship that it has begotten among us.[16]

Jesse Wilmore clearly articulated the response and the results of the revival period among Friends in the west.

> When the revival influence broke out,…we saw grand and glorious results coming to the church.…It was a time of rejoicing in the church's history. In this rejoicing it is no wonder that every and man every woman who had a gift from God pressed out to try to be an evangelist.…But only within the past few years has the church awakened to the fact that while we were gathering into the fold and bringing precious souls to accept Christ…by the hundreds, we were also getting into the church an element that was not strong, that was not able to help carry forward the interest of the church as it ought to be. We began to look around and see what was necessary, and the result has been on the other hand the cry from every place, almost, more ministerial help![17]

Howard Nicholson's affirmation of the pastoral system was rather unique. He challenged the contention that the hireling minister is only serving for money. As one who received financial support for his ministry, he said: "I dread the loss of the responsibility were my material support not dependent upon my gift in the ministry. I tell you it leads to faithfulness. I tell you when we know that we are supported and our families depend upon what is offered, it is an increased impetus and guard against physical laziness, against that continual desire to desert the cause for the work and all those things that deter ministerial effort."[18]

One other strong stand in favor of the pastoral system came from Barnabas Hobbs. His argument was quite biblical in nature as he discussed the words "elder," "shepherd," "overseer," "presbytery," "bishop," and "deacon" from the New Testament. He stressed the multi-leadership in the church fellowship which would prevent "one" person as pastor from becoming the authority.

One of the strongest reactions against came from Joseph Storrs Fry, an English Quaker.

> It is very possible that some of our older meetings and societies have been rather too slow in adopting new methods, and have not seen all that is capable of being done without transgressing anything that is a principle amongst us, but I am afraid that some of our Friends in some of the meetings, in endeavoring to meet a recognized want, have gone a little too far in the efforts of their loving zeal in endeavoring to bring all under the teaching of the Lord Jesus Christ, and I am afraid they have been involving themselves and the Society with which they are connected in some danger which, perhaps, they have not seen.[19]

As the time for Monday afternoon's session was drawing to a close, the Business Committee returned with a communication in regard to the subject of the ordinances. This was read and adopted by the Conference without discussion. The adopted report read as follows:

> A number of suggestions having been made by members of the Conference to the Business Committee, in reference to the teaching and practice of Water Baptism and the Supper, by those in official positions in the Society of Friends, the committee have given careful attention thereto, but believe that the recent official utterances, reaffirmations, and enactments of London Yearly Meeting, and of eight of the Yearly Meetings on this continent, in relation to Water Baptism and the Supper, have so definitely settled these questions in our branch of the Christian church, that there is no occasion for the discussion of them by this Conference.[20]

Monday evening's session resumed the discussion on the consideration of the ministry. Those Friends from the frontier yearly meetings which were beginning to integrate the pastoral system into the life of their yearly meeting were quite unapologetic about their new found freedom. It seemed to become apparent to the nonpastoral Friends that the "system" was here to stay. Some Friends from New York Yearly Meeting were also quite supportive. Mary Jane Weaver pointed out that Friends have always been supportive of traveling evangelists.

Benjamin Trueblood spoke next. He was another Iowa Quaker who spoke at length and built a strong biblical base for the pastoral system. He also built on Weaver's idea of the traveling evangelist: "Now, it is not clear to me at all why God's Spirit may guide one individual to travel in the ministry for a year, or five or six years, and receive thousands of dollars of money, and never work a day and do nothing but preach the Gospel—it is not clear to me why the Spirit of God should do that, and not guide in the selection of an individual who shall preach through an equal series of years in one place and Friends support him all that time."[21]

Another kind of argument for resisting the changes of pastoral ministry came from Sarah Clark of London. She appealed to the delegates that just as Friends are to be loyal to the Lord Jesus, they must also be loyal to His Church, which is the organizational body of Friends. "We must have organization for effective work. . . . I want to appeal to us all to be loyal to our organization."[22]

As Friends spoke in a straightforward manner and yet seemed to be listening to one another, David B. Updegraff realized that the discussion on ministry would actually give him an opportunity to appeal to Friends on considering other issues as well.

> I like this word flexibility. It has been a pet word with me for some time, a true, good, blessed word, and it belongs to the Society of Friends, and if it had not been for the flexibility that God has given us by the presence of His Spirit and the power of His truth, we would have been broken into a thousand fragments long ago.[23]

But Mary S. Thomas gave her idea about the meaning of the word "flexibility." This excerpt is one of the most interesting of the discussion considering the prophetic nature of her critique.

> I believe thoroughly in flexibility of methods, but I do not believe in flexibility of principles, and that is what I am pleading for tonight. We are standing on the principles, not on the method. . . Dear friends, if you let this method in,

and I believe in the bottom of my heart that it has nothing
to do with the Society of Friends at all, if you let it into
the church you will find the theological seminary at the end
of it.[24]

No one could have been better than Allen Jay in successfully bringing
this delicate discussion to a close.

I want to say that I unite on both sides of the question, but
at the same time there is something on both sides that I do
not unite with. . . .We have been told here to-night that
those congregations that had regular pastors have succeeded
in building up. . . .It has not been so where I have
observed. . . On the other hand, . . . it was not the fault of
the system so much as the fault of the man called to be
pastor. So there is a danger there, my friends, and we need
to watch on every hand. No system you can ever adopt will
be perfect unless you have perfect men and women to carry
it out. Consequently, to our brethren who are pleading so
much for the plan adopted by Iowa or Ohio or Indiana
Yearly Meeting, I would say, let none of them conclude
that they have a perfect system, and let none of them
conclude that there is no danger in it. Now, for my own
part, I believe that if we fall into the practice of having a
regular pastor, it will not be long until it will do away
with our women ministers. . . .One thing more: I trust that
what has been said here to-day in this long discussion will
all be gathered up; and we will think over it carefully, and
be careful, as we have heard here to-day, that in trying to
avoid the errors on the one hand we do not run into those
on the other hand, and, in the course of twenty-five years
from now, find ourselves in bondage on the other side of
the question.[25]

There was enough consensus during the discussion for the
"Conclusions" to have some meaning:

As the leading of the Lord's Spirit is faithfully followed,
there will be a right exercise of the liberty of the Gospel in
the ordering of our church work, but it is important that
those who are rightly occupying a prominent position in
our meetings should not become a separate order of men
and women, on whom the charge of the congregation would
be conferred, thus virutally excluding the gifts of other
brothers or sisters.[26]

The Conference
Concludes with a Declaration

The delegates gathered on Tuesday afternoon at 2:00 p.m. for their next to the last session. The plans were to discuss the question: "Would not some modification of our system of birthright membership be advisable?"[1]

However, the Business Committee recommended that a discussion on a proposed conference of yearly meetings should be taken up first. William Nicholson had been requested by the Business Committee to open the discussion of this question: "Shall we recommend the establishment of a Conference of Yearly Meetings, with certain delegated powers and to meet at stated periods?"[2] Nicholson argued the case in favor of such a gathering. He proposed a method and a twelve point plan to carry it out. He also recommended that the Yearly Meetings "unite in the formation of a delegate body of ultimate authority and appeal in all matters pertaining to Christian doctrine, discipline, and practice, and to be called The Triennial Meeting of the Religious Society of Friends."[3]

After Henry Hartshorne's remarks that William Nicholson was going too fast (perhaps such a conference could meet every five years and would not have ultimate authority to govern all the participating yearly meetings), it was decided to refer this proposition to the individual yearly meetings for discussion. A minute to this effect was included in the "Conclusions to the Conference."

> The proposition with reference to the establishment of a conference of Yearly Meetings, with certain delegated powers, to meet at stated periods, was considered, and the conference requests the Yearly Meetings to consider this subject.[4]

Then the Committee to Prepare a Declaration of Faith was given the floor. Joseph Bevan Braithwaite spoke on behalf of the committee: "Friends are aware of the pressure of time. We have endeavored as far as was possible to draw up that which might meet the case. We are very sensible that it has been under a good deal of pressure, and if it be entered upon, I do earnestly desire that it may be under a very serious and prayerful feeling."[5]

James Rhoads was asked to read the Declaration in two equal portions, one in the afternoon and the other in the evening session. It was then discussed according to each portion. Rhoads began the reading with this opening sentence: "It is under a deep sense of what we owe to Him who has loved us that we feel called upon to offer a declaration of those fundamental doctrines of Christian truth that have always been professed by our branch of the Church of Christ."[6] The declaration was categorized into sixteen sections of the Christian message as held by the traditional, Orthodox, Gurneyite, evangelical Quakers of the conference. Those sections were titled: God, the Lord Jesus Christ, the Holy Spirit, the Holy Scriptures, Man's Creation and Fall, Justification and Sanctification, the Resurrection and Final Judgment, Baptism, the Supper of the Lord, Public Worship, Prayer and Praise, Liberty to Conscience in Its Relation to Civil Government, Marriage, Peace, Oaths, the First Day of the Week. Almost all of these sections were at least touched upon during the deliberations in regard to the Declaration.

Before it was adopted by the conference, two things were made very clear. First, the document was drawn together from existing sources (scriptures, yearly meeting disciplines, earlier Quaker writings) and, therefore, it did not contain anything which had not already been expressed in some official document of one of the yearly meetings represented. It was intended to be an affirmation of faith which all of the yearly meetings could agree upon. Secondly, if adopted, it was not to supersede the affirmations which individual yearly meetings had already made, nor was it to interfere with the autonomy and independence of judgment of any of the yearly meetings.

This second clarification was made because David B. Updegraff pushed the question: ". . .is it the judgement of this Conference that each

Yearly Meeting should be left free in its own membership to exercise its own judgment and come to its own conclusions without undue pressure being brought to bear from members of other Yearly Meetings or from periodicals that suggest deplorable alternatives in case they do not do just as they are directed to do?"[7]

James Wood's response as Chairman of the Conference was as follows:

> The question of the Friend from Ohio is one that is clearly settled in the Society of Friends, that every Yearly Meeting is perfectly independent in its action, and is not influenced by any outside influence, except so far as the members submit to be influenced by light that comes to them.[8]

The discussions in regard to the Declaration tended to be scrutinizing at times. Charles Brady warned the Conference that "if we would begin to listen to detail criticisms such as we have listened to on the resurrection, we should find ourselves further apart rather than coming closer together."[9] David Updegraff picked up on this point and gave his strongest caution about adopting such a document:

> But I am about to remark, however, that concerning the latter part which we have heard, upon the matters of the baptism and the supper, I should be exceedingly glad if the course could be pursued with them that has been pursued with other matters that are treated of, the plain positive, affirmation upon the positive side of our apprehension of these matters. I as fully believe in the true spiritual nature and work, and only essential work, of the baptism of the Holy Ghost, and I should be glad for just as strong an affirmation to be made upon the positive side of that question as could be made, and also upon the positive side of the communion, the spiritual communion of the believer; but I make this plea for the dismission of that part of the report which is argumentative. . . .
>
> If this document goes down as it now stands, it is readily, I think, seen that it is open to the most minute scrutiny and investigation, and must inevitably lead to widely extended examination and debate. I do not believe that will be to the best interests of the church. I think if it is inevitable that it must go before the people for adoption or rejection, that to send down a document that would be rejected by some of

our Yearly Meetings, would be unfortunate. I do not think
that would be desired by any of us. To send down a
document that would have to be adopted by any of them
under pressure or coercion of conscience, I think that would
not be desirable, and I think the merits of this question are
more safely lodged in the hands of the church without the
discussion of this question, and its strong negations as
contained in the document.[10]

The only other strong concern about adopting the Declaration came
from Joseph Storrs Fry. His recommendation was to adopt the
Declaration "as generally expressing our views," and then submit it "for
the consideration of the Yearly Meetings."[11]

I have sat under a great deal of pressure of mind during the
whole afternoon and evening, with the feeling that there
was rather more haste than is quite wise in the proceedings
of a body representing so large a number of persons as are
practically represented here. I do not wish to introduce any
note of discord into a meeting which has been so
harmonious and pleasant, but I think I should have left the
meeting with a great deal of uncomfortable feeling, if I had
not been permitted, simply as an individual, to express my
thoughts. I only desire that we may not hastily commit
ourselves to any words which afterwards we might see
reason to desire to modify.[12]

The Declaration was not only seen as a means of providing unity
among the yearly meetings involved, but also as a stronger witness to
the world as to what Friends actually believed. John Henry Douglas
declared: "I believe, to take it as a whole, that it is the very best
document that we have ever produced for our church, and for the world,
from our people."[13]

Robert W. Douglas spoke with a similar sentiment as his brother:

It is in the good providence of the Lord that some of us
have to represent the Society of Friends outside of the
particular borders of local influence, and the great cry in
many of these places is that we are brought into contact
with a class of people who do not know the doctrines and
principles of the Society of Friends, and their question is,
What do Friends believe? and, although this document is
long, I do not see how we can make it shorter.[14]

Other delegates also agreed that this declaration was a document that could be effectively placed into the hands of inquirers about the Society of Friends. Many delegates hoped that the Declaration would give strength to the Society. Hannah Bailey of New England Yearly Meeting hoped that the Declaration would prevent any further Unitarianism from creeping into the Society. James Richardson of Dublin Yearly Meeting hoped that the Declaration would prevent Friends from verging off to the Methodists or some other denomination.

Many affirmations were given to the document, in general. And in the words of James Wood, the conference Chairman: "With great unanimity this Conference has adopted the Declaration of Faith that has been submitted."[15]

Many delegates expressed their joy in regard to the unity, fellowship, and love which was experienced in the Holy Spirit during the four days of the Conference. At the close Joseph Bevan Braithwaite gave his final exhortation:

> This being my fifth visit to this continent, the possibility of this being the last time of meeting many dearly beloved brothers and sisters, on this side of eternity, has come over me again and again; and it is not needful for me, for you all know it already, to say a great deal about how much my heart overflows with love.[16]

Epilogue

Responses to the Conference

The Richmond Conference of 1887 became history on September 28, 1887. The delegates of Indiana Yearly Meeting, working with the clerks, were responsible for the preparation, printing, and distribution of the transactions of the conference. They were also authorized by the conference to call upon the other yearly meetings to share in such expenses. This way thorough information could be distributed out among the family of Friends.

During the weeks, months, and even years, the responses to this historic event would keep rolling in. The responses would come from individuals, yearly meetings, Friends' periodicals, and conferences which would be held in the future.

INDIVIDUALS

"Everybody seems to believe that the Conference has done good," wrote Henry Hartshorne to Timothy Nicholson, the father of the Conference.[1] "Some are disappointed that no more *decisive action* was taken in regard to *Ohio*; but on reflection and information they can easily see that the Conference had neither *legislative* nor *executive* powers. I think, however, that D.B.U. gained some points in his own way."[2]

Soon after he returned home from the conference, James Rhoads wrote in a letter to another Philadelphia Friend, Samuel Morris, some reflections on the experience in Richmond:

> I had no wish to attend the Richmond Conference and went
> rather at the solicitation of my friends. But I believe the
> meetings turned out rather for the furtherance of the Gospel
> and the promotion of the Lord's kingdom. . . .I do not
> doubt that it would be better for us, and for the Society-at-
> large, had we always kept in open communication with all
> the Yearly Meetings.[3]

William Nicholson wrote his brother Timothy shortly after the
conference. The Kansas Yearly Meeting sessions were held after the
conference. William was grateful for the response of his yearly meeting
to the work of the conference. "When the work of the Conference was
laid before the meeting in joint session, ample time was given for full
and deliberate expression and it was overwhelmingly in favor of all that
the Conference did."[4]

Timothy Nicholson in a letter to Henry Hartshorne mentioned that he
"heard it stated that D.B.U. assumes that the actions of the Conference
settled the ordinances--and that now the Yearly Meetings that adopted
minutes excluding from their borders such ministers as he are now
legitimate fields for his services."[5]

YEARLY MEETINGS

Reports on the conference was found in all the minutes of ten of the
twelve participating yearly meetings.

The London Yearly Meeting minutes recorded the following:

> We have considered the Conclusions of the Conference, and
> the Declaration of Christian Truth, as held by Friends,
> adopted by it; both read in our separate Meetings yesterday--
> and receive them as faithfully reflecting the proceedings and
> views of the Conference. They are to be printed with the
> Proceedings of the Yearly Meeting, but inasmuch as this
> Meeting had no opportunity of entertaining the question of
> the need, for itself, of such a declaration, and has now no
> opportunity of revising that which has been presented; and
> inasmuch as many Friends have expressed an
> unwillingness, at the present time, to adopt any further
> declarations than those previously made and recorded as to
> our Christian faith, it is to be understood that, whilst re-
> affirming our adherence to the fundamental Scriptural
> doctrines always held by us, this Meeting refrains from

expressing any judgment on the contents of the Declaration now produced.[6]

Dublin Yearly Meeting recorded in their minutes:

Inasmuch as many Friends have expressed great and variety of judgment as to the adoption of this Declaration; and there having been, during this consideration, a large expression of thankfulness for the clear pronouncement contained therein, of fundamental truth, and of those things which are right to receive it as a valuable outcome of the Conference; and whilst this Meeting does not see its way formally to adopt it, we commend it to Friends in all our meetings.[7]

New England Yearly Meeting took the following action:

We accept the action of the Conference, and direct the publication of the "Declaration of Christian Doctrine" with our minutes.[8]

New York Yearly Meeting:

The document referred to was read, and after prayerful consideration accepted by the Meeting with entire unanimity as a True Declaration of Christian Doctrines held by the Religious Society of Friends.[9]

Baltimore Yearly Meeting:

The Conclusions of the Conference upon the subjects which claimed its attention, and the declaration of faith which it adopted have been read and approved by this Meeting.[10]

North Carolina Yearly Meeting:

We have considered the Declaration submitted and read in the meeting this morning, and directed it to be printed in the Minutes of this Meeting, adopting is as a valuable restatement of some of the fundamental doctrines of our Society.[11]

Nothing could be found in the minutes of Ohio Yearly Meeting which represented that yearly meeting as discussing or deliberating over the conference or the Declaration of Faith. Yet the delegates did give a brief report and the minutes record the following:

> It is our prayerful concern to uphold and to spread a knowledge of the truth and the fundamental doctrines of the gospel, and we gratefullly acknowledge the prevalence of a blessed unity in this endeavor. The "Conclusions of the Conference" and the Declaration of Faith are accepted as faithfully reflecting the proceedings and views of the Conference, and are printed for the information of our members and others.[12]

Indiana Yearly Meeting:

> The Conclusions of the Conference upon the various subjects which claimed its attention, and the Declaration of Faith which it adopted, have been read and are approved by this Meeting.[13]

Western Yearly Meeting:

> The Declaration of Faith prepared by the Conference has also been read, and after a full expression of sentiment we are united in accepting it as a statement of the Declaration of Faith of the Society of Friends, but not as a compulsory creed.[14]

Iowa Yearly Meeting:

> The delegates produced the statement of Christian Doctrine prepared by the Conference, which is approved by the Meeting as a general statement of the views of the Society of Friends upon the various subjects considered therein.[15]

Kansas Yearly Meeting:

> We have also read the summary of the Conclusions of the Conference alluded to in the Report, and the same is also approved by this Meeting.

We have also read the Declaration of Faith prepared by said Conference and approved the same. These documents will be inserted in the Minutes of this Meeting for the information and satisfaction of our members.[16]

Arthur Dorland in his *Quakers in Canada, A History* wrote about Canada Yearly Meeting's adoption of the Declaration of Faith:

In the resolution passed by Canada Yearly Meeting, in 1888, it was stated that the adoption of the Declaration was "not as a Creed, binding men's consciences, but as an Exposition of the Truth in Christ Jesus."[17]

Allen Thomas in his book, *A History of the Friends in America,* wrote within a few years of 1887 an interesting summary of the conference and particularly the Declaration of Faith.

The "Declaration" consisted largely of extracts from standard writings, and is too diffuse and general in its statements to be regarded as a rigid creed; nevertheless, it much more nearly approaches one than any of the Declarations that have preceded it. It conforms much more nearly to the standards of ordinary evangelical denominations. As might have been expected from the fact that baptism and the Supper were the questions then at issue, the space occupied in the consideration of these topics is disproportionately large. While it acknowledges the distinquishing views of Friends of the universality of the operation of the Spirit of Christ, it tends to pass them over. It states the Quaker doctrine of peace, and against oaths, etc., clearly and well; states in guarded language the doctrines of future rewards and punishments; and reaffirms the deity of Christ and salvation through him. The Declaration met with strong opposition in England, and London Yearly Meeting took no action on the document except to place it on its Minutes as part of the report of its committee. New England and Ohio took essentially the same position as London. Dublin, New York, and Baltimore gave it a general approval without adopting it. The other (Orthodox) Yearly Meetings in the United States adopted it. This variety of action in no way altered the official relations of the Yearly Meetings, for the action of the conference was only advisory and not authoritative.[18]

FRIENDS' PERIODICALS

In 1887 and 1888 there were many Friends' publications distributing information across Quakerism. Henry Hartshorne, for the *Friends' Review*, reported editorially: "The most important work accomplished was the preparation and adoption of a Declaration of Faith, recommended to the acceptance of all the Yearly Meetings...The trend or general bearing of the Conference was conservative, in the best sense of that word."[19]

A comparison of the *Review* with *The Christian Worker* reveals that the discussions and conclusions perhaps yielded some ambivalence as to whether the tone was "conservative" or "liberal": "It was plain that in number, in strength of argument, and in practical results for good, the liberal branch was the stronger, and that this cause has gained by the discussion."[20]

From *The Friend*, Philadelphia's conservative periodical, one can find these reactions to the Richmond Conference.

> If the judgment of *The Christian Worker* is correct, that what it terms the "liberal" cause gained ground in the Conference, and that meetings can feel that they may make special arrangements for pastoral provision, with the consciousness that they are *in harmony with the voice of the Conference*; the hopes of those lovers of our principles who looked for any real good to result of the meeting of this body will be sadly disappointed. For the re-affirmation of our views on the ordinances is of little importance compared with the preservation of our meetings and our ministry on their ancient foundation.[21]

> The more we have reflected upon the proceedings of the late Conference of Yearly Meetings at Richmond, Indiana, the more decided have become our fear that its influence in the Society of Friends will be more largely for evil than for good.[22]

Conservative Friends would have seen the Friends at the Richmond Conference drifting further toward liberalism by allowing pastoral systems, congregational singing, and programmed meetings for worship. "It is much to be regretted that the number and influence of these were not sufficient to so shape the proceedings of the Conference as to relieve the difficulties and fear of those 'conservative' members who have felt themselves unable to work in harmony with the new principles and practices of latter times."[23]

Benjamin Trueblood wrote an article for *The Christian Worker* entitled "Creeds and Conferences." In it he distinquishes the difference between a creed and a declaration of faith.

> A creed stands for that which is much more "hard and fast," . . .A creed once made and signed is hard to change. . . .A Declaration of Faith . . .is a much simpler affair. It is more elastic and capable of being adapted to the growing necessities of the individual and the church. . . .It can be reconstructed every time the individual or the church comes into possession of new light which gives a wider and clearer conception of truth. It requires no subscription except that of an honest heart. . . .it shows devout respect for all that is now known of the truth of God, but leaves the way open for all deeper and truer comprehension of it. . . .If written Declarations were not made, oral ones would appear and be handed down.[24]

The criticism from the *Friends' Intelligencer and Journal* agreed with *The Friend* that the Richmond Conference drifted away from the heart of the movement of the early Friends. However, the concern is not as much over forms and practices but in the area of theology instead.

> The name of George Fox or any other of the early Friends is not introduced, and there is no allusion to them as authorities as to what has "always been professed by Friends."
>
> There is not, as far as we can observe, any distinct presentation of the fundamental principles declared by Goerge Fox and his immediate followers: the Indwelling Light.[25]

The Friends' Quarterly Examiner can give one a slight glimpse as to why London Yearly Meeting didn't adopt the Declaration.

> Whatever views may be entertained with regard to this Conference and its conclusions, it is impossible for any thoughtful person to read through the Stenographic Report without being sensible of the life and earnestness of the Society of Friends in America, and their anxiety to grapple with the problems of actual life as they find them to exist around them. . .

The truth of progressive Revelation is becoming more and more recognized by thoughtful Christians. In all departments of scientific discovery we find advance, and yet the truths that are being discovered are what they always have been. It is simply that fuller *insight* has been given into their meaning.

The Society of Friends has been specially privileged in having no creed but Scripture, and although it may be said that the "Declaration" is mainly in the words of Scripture, yet we cannot fail to see the distinction between the concentration of various doctrines here and the beautiful freedom from any rigid forms in the Sacred writings. In the Bible we have truth presented in a great variety of ways, often apparent paradoxes, yet all really consistent with each other; all seeming "discord being not understood."[26]

After reviewing and affirming most of the discussions and conclusions of the conference, *The Friend* (London) expressed its concerns about the conference.

Hitherto our remarks have implied general and cordial unity with the work and spirit of the Conference. But although it may appear presumptuous, it would be dishonest of us if we were to express anything short of great uneasiness in regard to its treatment of two other questions which occupied its attention. . . We refer to the question of making the Conference a permanent institution, and to the issuing of a declaration of faith.

Having issued this "Declaration of Faith," the Conference "submit it to the Yearly Meetings represented for their consideration and approval." This will bring very grave responsibility upon them all, and suggests many difficult questions: but we have said enough for the present.[27]

Two letters-to-the-editor in *The British Friend* give more reasons why London Yearly Meeting was not ready to adopt another declaration. George Milne reminded Friends that "many passages in the Declaration were taken from the Epistles of London Yearly Meeting. It should, however, be borne in mind, that those Epistles are not passed with the same care that would be necessary in adopting a Declaration of Faith."[28]

William Pollard, another English Friend, wrote another letter-to-the-editor of *The British Friend*:

> In 1872 the Lancashire Committee of the Yearly
> Meeting, in presenting their final report, appended a
> Declaration of Faith, which though not nearly so diffuse, is
> in many respects identical with the paper adopted at
> Richmond. At the Yearly Meeting of 1872 the proposal to
> adopt this declaration was carefully considered, and a
> number of earnest Friends were desirous that such a step
> should be taken. But after full deliberation this proposal
> was definitely set aside.[29]

No Friends' periodical gave more copy space to the Richmond
Conference than David B. Updegraff and his *Friends' Expositor*. He
sought to give a fairly objective overview of the Conference before he
began his critical editorial work.

> If the doctrines held by us are found in the Holy Scriptures,
> and revealed to us through the Holy Spirit, then they are
> the heritage of all the children of God, and they are
> doubtless revealed to us to make them known, so that
> others may have a like blessing with ourselves. Popes,
> Councils and Synods have formulated "Creeds," but what
> does history record as the result? The Creeds of the Church
> for centuries were little better than the death warrants of the
> faithful followers of the Lord, who would not obey the
> "commandments of men," and the formulae of the Church
> in past ages have been stained with the blood of martyrs,
> instruments of persecution and the bulwarks of ignorance,
> bigotry, intolerance and superstition.

> History repeats itself; and though the result may differ in
> degree, I have little doubt that if the Society of Friends
> adopts the Richmond "declaration of faith" there are those
> amongst us who will try to use the formula to enforce
> restrictions and inflict disabilities on those who cannot
> conscientiously subscribe to every article, and those Friends
> will be creating an instrument whereby enemies of progress
> may keep the Church in a state of constant warfare and
> unrest, and hinder its real work.[30]

FUTURE CONFERENCES

Two of the considerations which came before the Richmond Conference of 1887 would eventually bring a number of the yearly meetings back together. Those were the union of the yearly meetings in the foreign missionary work and the proposal for the establishment of a Triennial Conference of yearly meetings with delegated powers.

A second Conference was held in Indianapolis in 1892, having been preceded by a preliminary Conference in Oskaloosa, Iowa, in 1891. A third Conference was held in 1897. This gathering recommended the formation of a central body of American yearly meetings to manage possible unified activites which included missions. William Nicholson's vision for such a Conference was being realized. However, this body would not have the ultimate delegated authority to the extreme that Nicholson visualized as necessary. The central body was established in 1902 by eleven of the Orthodox yearly meetings. The Five Years Meeting, now Friends United Meeting, united on the basis of the Uniform Discipline which was considered the common declaration of faith, constitution of government and rules of discipline. Included in the Uniform Discipline was the Richmond Declaration of Faith as well as George Fox's letter to the Governor of Barbadoes and a statement called "Essential Truths." Those yearly meetings which adopted the Uniform Discipline and became an official part of the Five Years Meeting in 1902 were New England, New York, Baltimore, North Carolina, Indiana, Western, Iowa, Wilmington, Kansas, Oregon, and California.

> Despite the widespread criticism of the "Richmond Declaration," in England and the more conservative sections of American Quakerism, it did serve to unite those sections which were undergoing the stresses of change and expansion. It aroused a spirit of unity and common interest on the part of many Friends and led to the formation of the Five Years Meeting.[31]

Reflections
One Hundred Years Later

The Richmond Conference of 1887 was a gathering of passionate followers of Jesus Christ who were willing to struggle with the issues and questions of faith in their day. With the exception of the discussion of the ordinances, the conference was an open and rigorous dialogue of candor, intensity, and respect. Even in reading the proceedings one hundred years later, one can capture a feeling of the authenticity of the lives of these diligent Quakers. The decision to not discuss the ordinances even seemed to be a matter of integrity. It prevented the explosive potential of that subject from dominating the time together.

This sense of asking the questions and struggling with the issues provided a healthy atmosphere for the conference. There are probably several reasons why this was so. First of all, this was a group of people who individually had a deep hunger for God and sought to walk daily in the Spirit. Their reminiscences, journals, writings, autobiographies, and biographies written about them all reveal their passion to be servants of God. They brought this commitment with them, and, therefore, the discussions were permeated with worship. They centered to seek guidance and a clear vision from God for witness and unity.

Secondly, they spoke with such honesty because they did have a great deal of freedom. They knew the importance of experiencing harmony in their relationships as individuals and yearly meetings, but until that time they were not officially or institutionally committed to one another. They respectfully spoke the truth as they understood it without the burden of maintaining an organization.

Third, for the most part and in line with the best of Quaker tradition, they shared out of their own experience. The years of revivalism of the frontier following the Civil War offered fresh, experiential religion for seekers in several denominations. Many Friends welcomed this emphasis of the inner workings of the Spirit in the life of the believer. Much of their discussion at the conference centered around their experience with God or with the seekers of God. Though their theology was often Bible-oriented and primarily orthodox in regard to the history of the Christian movement, they sought to speak theologically in a way that was a reflection of their relationship with God. They seemed to respect the authenticity of each other's faith as it was related from personal experience.

In essence, the questions and issues of the Richmond Conference of 1887 still face the Religious Society of Friends today. What is the message and mission of the Society of Friends? How can we best declare this message to the world and fulfill this mission? Is a union of yearly meetings in mission work, service, witness, and ministry desirable? How should Friends experience and conduct their meetings for worship? How do Friends understand the meaning and experience of baptism and communion? What is the relation of the ministry to the church and the church to the ministry? How shall the ministry be sustained? Is it desirable that all yearly meetings adopt one common declaration of faith?

Worship, ministry, the sacraments, faith statements, outreach and the larger "calling" upon the Society of Friends are vital concerns which need continuing dialogue today. Members of each generation must ask their questions and struggle with their issues individually and with each other in order to live out an authentic faith. Each larger question generates particular questions, evident in the issue of ministry alone.

One hundred years ago some Friends were concerned that the ministry of women would be diminished if a paid pastoral system was adopted in a society that was oriented around males as the wage-earners of the day. They were prophetic. At the turn of the century more than one-third of the pastors, recorded ministers, and missionaries in the yearly meetings of the Five Years Meeting were women. The number of women today is a small fraction of what it was. What are we doing to nurture the pastoral ministry of women today? As pastors settled down in communities and meetings, the role of the traveling minister also diminished. Was the prophetic ministry weakened when the freedom of the traveling minister to speak "the word of the Lord," call Friends' lives into account by updating the testimonies, or remind Friends of the larger picture of the world was gone? Did the historic distinctives of peace, simplicity, integrity, and equality merely become personal matters as the "paid" pastor began to feel uncomfortable making his or her congregation uncomfortable? Did the spiritual gifts of others in the meeting go unrecognized and unaffirmed as Friends allowed the "released" ministers to tend to all the needs of the meeting? Did evangelism and social concern begin to have divergent paths as Friends began to prioritize the importance of such ministries? Similar questions could be asked of non-pastoral Friends in regard to the recognition of spiritual gifts, the nurture of various needs in the meeting, etc. Do we even admit that such questions are legitimate? Do we allow Friends to wrestle with these issues of ministry today? How open and honest are we to dialogue with other Friends in order to see a bigger picture of God's vision and love for the world?

As I have given much consideration to the Richmond Conference of 1887 and its subsequent Declaration of Faith, I have seemed to hear Christ Jesus say to me, "So now you know what Joseph Bevan Braithwaite, James Rhoads, Esther Frame, Benjamin Trueblood, and ninety-five other Quakers who gathered in Richmond, Indiana, in September of 1887 said about me; but my question to you is, 'But what about you? Who do you say I am?' "[1]

As Friends in 1887 sought to have a living faith and a vital relationship with Christ in their day, so I am challenged to experience my own faith and relationship with Christ in my day in community with other Friends. Their story, like so many other stories in Quaker history, as well as in the history of the universal Church, can give some encouragement and shed some light on my path. But the only moment in which I can experience God through love and service is this moment. May my faith and the faith of Friends today be such a living faith.

Notes

Chapter 1

1. Howard H. Brinton, *Friends for 300 Years* (Wallingford, Pennsylvania: Pendle Hill Publications, 1965), p. 66.

2. Elbert Russell, *The History of Quakerism* (Richmond, Indiana: Friends United Press, 1979), pp. 282-291.

3. Rufus M. Jones, *The Later Periods of Quakerism*, vol. ii (London: MacMillan and Company, Ltd., 1921), p. 462.

4. Russell, *The History of Quakerism*, pp. 322-323.

5. Arthur J. Mekeel, *Quakerism and a Creed* (Philadelphia: Friends Book Store, 1936), p. 62.

6. Edward Grubb, *Separations: Their Causes and Effects* (London: Headley Brothers, 1914), pp. 45-46.

7. Russell, *The History of Quakerism*, p. 348.

8. Grubb, *Separations: Their Causes and Effects*, p. 93.

9. Richard Wood, "The Rise of Semi-Structured Worship," in *Quaker Worship*, ed. Fran Hall, (Richmond, Indiana: Friends United Press, 1978), pp. 56-57.

10. Allen Jay, *Autobiography of Allen Jay* (Philadelphia: The John C. Winston Company, 1910), p. 81.

Chapter 2

1. Jones, *The Later Periods of Quakerism*, p. 896.
2. Mary Coffin Johnson, ed., *Rhoda M. Coffin: Her Reminiscenses* (New York: Grafton Press, 1910), pp. 79-80.
3. Jones, *The Later Periods of Quakerism*, pp. 894-895.
4. Ibid., p. 893.
5. Ibid., p. 896.
6. Johnson, *Rhoda M. Coffin*, p. 81.
7. A. H. Votaw, "Allen Jay," in *Quaker Biographies*, ser. ii, vol. III (Philadelphia: Friends Book Store, 1920), pp. 77-78.
8. Johnson, *Rhoda M. Coffin*, p. 81.
9. William J. Allison, ed., *Friends' Review* 14 (October 1860), p. 104.
10. Johnson, *Rhoda M. Coffin*, p. 81.
11. William J. Allison, ed., *Friends' Review* 14 (October 1860), pp. 104-105.
12. Errol T. Elliot, *Quakers on the American Frontier* (Richmond, Indiana: Friends United Press, 1969), p. 381.
13. Darius B. Cook, *Memoirs of Quaker Divide* (Dexter, Iowa: The Dexter Sentinel, 1914), p. 66.
14. Jones, *The Later Periods of Quakerism*, pp. 900-901.
15. Ibid., p. 901.
16. Minute, New York Yearly Meeting, 1871.
17. Cook, *Memoirs of Quaker Divide*, p. 67.
18. Minute, Iowa Yearly Meeting, 1872.

Chapter 3

1. Minute, Western Yearly Meeting, 1870.
2. Minute, Baltimore Yearly Meeting, 1870.
3. Ibid.
4. Minute, London Yearly Meeting, 1871.
5. Henry Hartshorne, ed., *Friends' Review* 29 (October 1875), p. 105.
6. Ibid.
7. Minute, Western Yearly Meeting, 1875.

Chapter 4

1. Anna Braithwaite Thomas, *J. Bevan Braithwaite: A Friend of the Nineteenth Century* (London: Hodder and Stoughton, 1909), p. 32.

2. Ibid.

3. Ibid., p. 27.

4. Ibid., pp. 64-65.

5. Jones, *The Later Periods of Quakerism*, p. 908.

6. Thomas, *J. Bevan Braithwaite*, pp. 74-75.

7. "Friends Ancient and Modern," no. 8, *Joseph Bevan Braithwaite* (New York: David S. Taber, 1906), p. 9.

8. Ibid., p. 10.

9. Thomas, *J. Bevan Braithwaite*, p. 122.

10. R. C. Scott, "Authority or Experience," *The Journal of the Friends' Historical Society* 49 (Spring 1960), p. 79.

11. Grubb, *Separations: Their Causes and Effects*, p. 124.

Chapter 5

1. Walter C. Woodward, *Timothy Nicholson: Master Quaker* (Richmond, Indiana: The Nicholson Press, 1927), p. 30.

2. Charles E. Tebbetts, *Biographical Sketch of the Late William Nicholson, M.D.* (Richmond, Indiana: Nicholson Printing and Manufacturing Company, 1909), p. 5.

3. Jones, *The Later Periods of Quakerism*, p. 939.

4. Woodward, *Timothy Nicholson: Master Quaker*, p. 84.

5. Jones, *The Later Periods of Quakerism*, p. 939.

6. Elliot, *Quakers on the American Frontier*, p. 105.

7. Woodward, *Timothy Nicholson: Master Quaker*, p. 139.

8. Ibid., pp. 189-190.

Chapter 6

1. Jay, *Autobiography of Allen Jay*, pp. 84-85.

2. Ibid., p. 85.

3. J. Brent Bill, *David B. Updegraff: Quaker Holiness Preacher* (Richmond, Indiana: Friends United Press, 1983), p. 16.

4. Ibid., p. 17.

5. Russell, *The History of Quakerism*, p. 487.

6. Edwin B. Bronner, ed., *An English View of American Quakerism: The Journal of Walter Robson, 1877* (Philadelphia: American Philosophical Society, 1970), p. 41.

7. Ibid., p. 84.

8. Minute, Ohio Yearly Meeting, 1879.

9. David C. LeShana, *Quakers in California: The Effects of 19th*

Century Revivalism on Western Quakerism (Newberg, Oregon: The Barclay Press, 1979), p. 60.

10. Bronner, *An English View of American Quakerism*, p. 104.

11. Henry Hartshorne, Letter to D. B. Updegraff, 9 Oct. 1875; Hartshorne Papers, Quaker Collection, Haverford College, Haverford, Pennsylvania.

12. Russell, *The History of Quakerism*, p. 488.

13. Bill, *David B. Updegraff*, p. 25.

14. Timothy Nicholson, Letter to Raymer Kelsey, 2 Aug. 1910; Nicholson Papers, Lilly Library, Earlham College, Richmond, Indiana.

Chapter 7

1. Paul J. Furnas, "Allen Jay: 1831-1910" (Lecture delivered at the 50th Anniversary of the West Richmond Friends Meeting; Richmond, Indiana, 1959), p. 14.

2. Ibid.

3. Jay, *Autobiography of Allen Jay*, p. 23.

4. Ibid., pp. 80-81.

5. Ibid., p. 24.

6. Ibid., p. 209.

Chapter 8

1. Elizabeth A. Cox, "Memorial of John Henry Douglas", in "Documents Dealing with the Life and Work of John Henry Douglas, Quaker Evangelist 1832-1919"; Lilly Library Vault, Earlham College, Richmond, Indiana; p. 3.

2. Bronner, *An English View of American Quakerism*, p. 90.

3. Minute, Iowa Yearly Meeting, 1888.

4. LaShana, *Quakers in California*, p. 135.

5. Cox, "Memorial of John Henry Douglas", pp. 6 & 8.

Chapter 9

1. Hannah Whitall Smith, *John M. Whitall: The Story of His Life* (Philadelphia: Printed for the family, 1879), pp. 180-181.

2. Ibid., pp. 184-185.

3. Ibid., pp. 181-182.

4. Ibid., pp. 213-214.

5. Ibid., p. 221.

6. Anna Braithwaite Thomas, *Richard H. Thomas, M.D.* (Philadelphia: The John C. Winston Company, 1905), pp. 167-168.

7. Ibid., pp. 218, 220-221.

8. Ibid., p. 219.

Chapter 10

1. Esther G. Frame and Nathan T. Frame, *Reminiscences* (Cleveland: Britton Printing Company, 1907), p. 68.

2. Ibid., p. 30.

3. Ibid., p. 27.

4. Ibid., p. 32.

5. Ibid., p. 35.

6. Ibid., p. 33.

7. Ibid., p. 38.

8. Bronner, *An English View of American Quakerism,* pp. 43-44.

9. Frame, *Reminiscences,* p. 84.

10. Ibid., p. 82.

11. Ibid., p. 107.

12. Ibid., p. 79.

13. Ibid., pp. 92-93.

14. Ibid., p. 209.

15. Ibid., p. 424.

Chapter 11

1. Charles Beals, *Benjamin F. Trueblood: Prophet of Peace* (New York: Friends Book and Tract Committee, 1916), p. 20.

2. Edwin D. Mead, "Introduction," *The Development of the Peace Idea and Other Essays,* ed. Sarah S. Trueblood (Norwood, Massachusettes: Plimptom Press, 1932), p. xx.

3. Jones, *The Later Periods of Quakerism,* p. 757.

4. Beals, *Benjamin F. Trueblood,* p. 4.

5. James Rhoads, Letter to Benjamin Trueblood, 25 Sept. 1888; Rhoads Papers, Quaker Collection, Haverford College, Haverford, Pennsylvania.

6. James Rhoads, Letter to Benjamin Trueblood, 31 July 1894; Rhoads Papers, Quaker Collection, Haverford College, Haverford, Pennsylvania.

7. Benjamin Trueblood, "The Twentienth Century Friend and His Bible School," *The American Friend* 2 (July 1895), pp. 574-578.

Chapter 12

1. Bronner, *An English View of American Quakerism*, p. 14.
2. Cook, *Memoirs of Quaker Divide*, pp. 70-71.
3. Ibid., p. 79.
4. Bronner, *An English View of American Quakerism*, pp. 56-57.
5. Ibid., pp. 57-58.
6. Ibid., pp. 68-69.
7. Ibid., pp. 71-72.
8. Daniel Hill, ed., *The Christian Worker* 12 (Sept. 1877), p. 615.
9. Henry Hartshorne, Letter to Dougan Clark, 8 Sept. 1883; Hartshorne Papers, Quaker Collection, Haverford College, Haverford, Pennsylvania.
10. Henry Hartshorne, Letter to David Updegraff, 9 Oct. 1875; Hartshorne Papers, Quaker Collection, Haverford College, Haverford, Pennsylvania.
11. Henry Hartshorne, Letter to David Updegraff, Nov. 1875; Hartshorne Papers, Quaker Collection, Haverford College, Haverford, Pennsylvania.
12. Henry Hartshorne, Letter to David Updegraff, 6 Feb. 1875; Hartshorne Papers, Quaker Collection, Haverford College, Haverford, Pennsylvania.
13. James Rhoads and Henry Hartshorne, Letter to Friends, 15 May 1883; Hartshorne Papers, Quaker Collection, Haverford College, Haverford, Pennsylvania.

Chapter 13

1. Minute, Ohio Yearly Meeting, 1879.
2. Ibid.
3. Ibid.
4. Ibid.
5. Ibid.
6. David B. Updegraff, "The Light Within," *Friends' Review* 32 (April 1879), p. 563.
7. Ibid.
8. Ibid.
9. Ibid., p. 562.

10. James E. Rhoads, ed., *Friends' Review* 32 (April 1879), p. 563.

11. Ibid., p. 569.

12. Ibid.

13. Joseph Walton, ed., *The Friend* 52 (April 1879), p. 286.

14. Ibid.

15. Joseph Braithwaite, Letter to Joseph Taylor, 27 Aug. 1878; Taylor Papers, Quaker Collection, Haverford College, Haverford, Pennsylvania.

16. John Greenleaf Whittier, "Letter to the Editor," *The Friend* 52 (May 1879), p. 327.

17. Henry Hartshorne, Letters to David Updegraff, 17 & 18 Jan. 1876; Hartshorne Papers, Quaker Collection, Haverford College, Haverford, Pennsylvania.

18. Ibid.

19. Henry Hartshorne, Letter to John Henry Douglas, 26 April 1884; Hartshorne Papers, Quaker Collection, Haverford College, Haverford, Pennsylvania.

20. Ibid.

21. Ibid.

Chapter 14

1. Bill, *David B. Updegraff*, p. 26.

2. Ibid., p. 31.

3. Minute, Indiana Yearly Meeting, 1886.

4. Henry Hartshorne, Letter to the Editors of the *Christian Union*, 1879; Hartshorne Papers, Quaker Collection, Haverford College, Haverford, Pennsylvania.

5. Henry Hartshorne, Letter to the Editor of the *Christian Witness*, 10 Sept. 1885; Hartshorne Papers, Quaker Collection, Haverford College, Haverford, Pennsylvania.

6. Ibid.

7. Ibid.

8. Israel P. Hole, Letter to Timothy Nicholson, 27 Sept. 1886; Nicholson Papers, Lilly Library Vault, Earlham College, Richmond, Indiana.

9. Henry Hartshorne, Letter to David Updegraff, 28 Oct. 1886; Hartshorne Papers, Quaker Collection, Haverford College, Haverford, Pennsylvania.

Chapter 15

1. Benjamin Trueblood, "Ministers' Wages," *The Christian Worker* 2 (Sept. 1872), p. 173.

2. Ibid.

3. Ibid.

4. Benjamin Trueblood, "Ministers' Wages," *The Christian Worker* 2 (Oct. 1872), p. 186.

5. Ibid., p. 187.

6. Daniel Hill, ed., *The Christian Worker* 12 (Sept. 1877), p. 615.

7. Ibid.

8. Wood, "The Rise in Semi-Structured Worship," p. 67.

9. Minute, Iowa Yearly Meeting, 1887.

10. Minute, Iowa Yearly Meeting, 1890.

11. Henry Hartshorne, ed., *Friends' Review* 40 (Jan. 1887), p. 408.

12. Ibid.

13. John Henry Douglas, Letter to Henry Hartshorne, 10 Feb. 1887; Hartshorne Papers, Quaker Collection, Haverford College, Haverford, Pennsylvania.

14. Henry Hartshorne, Letter to John H. Douglas, 12 Feb. 1887; Hartshorne Papers, Quaker Collection, Haverford College, Haverford, Pennsylvania.

Chapter 16

1. Timothy Nicholson, Letter to Calvin Pritchard, 29 Oct. 1885; Nicholson Papers, Lilly Library Vault, Earlham College, Richmond, Indiana.

2. Woodward, *Timothy Nicholson: Master Quaker*, p. 182.

3. Ibid., p. 189.

4. Minute, Indiana Yearly Meeting, 1886.

5. Timothy Nicholson, Letter to James Rhoads, 14 March 1887; Nicholson Papers, Lilly Library Vault, Earlham College, Richmond, Indiana.

6. Ibid.

7. Timothy Nicholson, Letter to James Rhoads, 7 July 1887; Hartshorne Papers, Quaker Collection, Haverford College, Haverford, Pennsylvania.

8. David B. Updegraff, *Friends Expositor* (July 1887), p. 65.

9. Ibid.

10. Ibid.

158

11. Ibid.

12. William Nicholson, Letter to Henry Hartshorne and James Rhoads, 10 Sept. 1887; Hartshorne Papers, Quaker Collection, Haverford College, Haverford, Pennsylvania.

13. Joseph Walton, ed., *The Friend* 60 (May 1887), p. 318.

14. Henry Hartshorne, Letter to J. Sewell, 28 Aug. 1887; Hartshorne Papers, Quaker Collection, Haverford College, Haverford, Pennsylvania.

15. W. L. Pearson, Letter to Timothy Nicholson, 15 Sept. 1887; Nicholson Papers, Lilly Library Vault, Earlham College, Richmond, Indiana.

16. William Nicholson, Letter to Timothy Nicholson, June 1887; Nicholson Papers, Lilly Library Vault, Earlham College, Richmond, Indiana.

17. William Nicholson, Letter to Timothy Nicholson, 20 Sept. 1887; Nicholson Papers, Lilly Library Vault, Earlham College, Richmond, Indiana.

Chapter 17

1. Allen Jay; Mahalah Jay; and Thomas N. White, ed., *Proceedings, including Declaration of Christian Doctrine, of the General Conference of Friends, held in Richmond, Indiana, U.S.A., 1887* (Richmond, Indiana: Nicholson & Bro., 1887), p. 3.

2. Ibid., pp. 44-45.

3. Ibid., p. 10.

4. Ibid., p. 9.

5. Ibid.

6. Ibid., p. 11.

7. Ibid., p. 12.

8. Ibid., p. 14.

9. Ibid., pp. 18-21.

10. Ibid., p. 55.

11. Ibid., p. 58.

12. Ibid., p. 60.

13. Ibid., p. 65.

14. Ibid.

15. Ibid.

16. Ibid., pp. 90-91.

17. Ibid., p. 104.

18. Ibid., p. 19.
19. Ibid., p. 105.
20. Ibid., pp. 19-20.
21. Ibid., p. 119.
22. Ibid., p. 115.
23. Ibid., p. 127.
24. Ibid., pp. 131-132.
25. Ibid., p. 133.
26. Ibid.

Chapter 18

1. Jay, *Proceedings of Friends Conference 1887*, p. 135.
2. Ibid., p. 137.
3. Ibid., p. 140.
4. Ibid., p. 152.
5. Ibid., p. 159.
6. Ibid., p. 172.
7. Ibid., p. 14.
8. Ibid., p. 179.
9. Ibid., p. 180.
10. Thomas, *J. Bevan Braithwaite*, pp. 319-321.
11. Woodward, *Timothy Nicholson: Master Quaker*, pp. 191-192.
12. Jay, *Autobiography of Allen Jay*, pp. 361-362.
13. Jay, *Proceedings of Friends Conference 1887*, pp. 181-182.
14. Ibid., p. 188.
15. Ibid., pp. 189-190.
16. Ibid., p. 215.
17. Ibid., pp. 216-217.
18. Ibid., p. 219.
19. Ibid., pp. 223-224.
20. Ibid., p. 15.
21. Ibid., p. 231.
22. Ibid., p. 241.
23. Ibid., p. 247.
24. Ibid., pp. 253-254.
25. Ibid., pp. 256-258.
26. Ibid., p. 22.

Chapter 19

1. Jay, *Proceedings of Friends Conference 1887*, p. 262.
2. Ibid., p. 263.
3. Ibid., p. 266.
4. Ibid., p. 23.
5. Ibid., p. 275.
6. Ibid., p. 24.
7. Ibid., p. 306.
8. Ibid., p. 307.
9. Ibid., p. 281.
10. Ibid., pp. 281-282.
11. Ibid., p. 302.
12. Ibid.
13. Ibid., pp. 279-280.
14. Ibid., p. 285.
15. Ibid., p. 309.
16. Ibid., p. 322.

Chapter 20

1. Woodward, *Timothy Nicholson: Master Quaker*, p. 193.
2. Henry Hartshorne, Letter to Timothy Nicholson, 25 Oct. 1887; Nicholson Papers, Lilly Library Vault, Earlham College, Richmond, Indiana.
3. James Rhoads, Letter to Samuel Morris, 4 Oct. 1887; Morris Papers, Quaker Collection, Haverford College, Haverford, Pennsylvania.
4. William Nicholson, Letter to Timothy Nicholson, 17 Oct. 1887; Nicholson Papers, Lilly Library Vault, Earlham College, Richmond, Indiana.
5. Timothy Nicholson, Letter to Henry Hartshorne, 28 Jan. 1888; Hartshorne Papers, Quaker Collection, Haverford College, Haverford, Pennsylvania.
6. Minute, London Yearly Meeting, 1888.
7. Minute, Dublin Yearly Meeting, 1888.
8. Minute, New England Yearly Meeting, 1888.
9. Minute, New York Yearly Meeting, 1888.
10. Minute, Baltimore Yearly Meeting, 1887.
11. Minute, North Carolina Yearly Meeting, 1888.
12. Minute, Ohio Yearly Meeting, 1888.

13. Minute, Indiana Yearly Meeting, 1887.

14. Minute, Western Yearly Meeting, 1888.

15. Minute, Iowa Yearly Meeting, 1888.

16. Minute, Kansas Yearly Meeting, 1887.

17. Arthur G. Dorland, *The Quakers in Canada, A History* (Toronto: the Ryerson Press, 1968), P. 265.

18. Allen C. Thomas, *A History of Friends in America* (Philadelphia: The John C. Winston Company, 1919), pp. 198-199.

19. Henry Hartshorne, ed., *Friends' Review* 41 (Oct. 1887), p. 152.

20. Calvin Pritchard, ed., *The Christian Worker* 17 (Oct. 1887), p. 474.

21. Joseph Walton, ed., *The Friend* 61 (Oct. 1887), p. 95.

22. Joseph Walton, ed., *The Friend* 61 (Nov. 1887), p. 111.

23. Ibid., p. 112.

24. Benjamin Trueblood, "Creeds and Conferences," *The Christian Worker* 18 (March 1888), p. 133.

25. *Friends' Intelligencer and Journal* 44 (Oct. 1887), p. 685.

26. Richard Westlake, ed., *The Friends' Quarterly Examiner* 86 (April 1888), pp. 145, 148-149.

27. *The Friend* (London) 27 (Nov. 1887), pp. 279-281.

28. George Milne, "Letter to the Editor," *The British Friend* (May 1888), p. 116.

29. William Pollard, "Letter to the Editor," *The British Friend* (May 1888), p. 117.

30. David B. Updegraff, ed., *Friends Expositor* 2 (April 1888), pp. 127-128.

31. Mekeel, *Quakerism and a Creed*, pp. 108-109.

Chapter 21

1. Mark 8:29 (New International Version).

Bibliography

BOOKS

Baltzell, E. Digby. *Puritan Boston and Quaker Philadelphia*. Boston: Beacon Press, 1979.

Beals, Charles. *Benjamin F. Trueblood: Prophet of Peace*. New York: Friends Book and Tract Committee, 1916.

Bill, J. Brent. *David B. Updegraff: Quaker Holiness Preacher*. Richmond, Indiana: Friends United Press, 1983.

Brinton, Howard H. *Friends For 300 Years*. Wallingford, Pennsylvania: Pendle Hill Publications, 1965.

Bronner, Edwin B., ed. *An English View of American Quakerism: The Journal of Walter Robson, 1877*. Philadelphia: American Philosophical Society, 1970.

Cook, Darius B. *Memoirs of Quaker Divide*. Dexter, Iowa: The Dexter Sentinel, 1914.

Dorland, Arthur G. *The Quakers in Canada, A History*. Toronto: The Ryerson Press, 1968.

Elliott, Errol T. *Quakers on the American Frontier*. Richmond, Indiana: Friends United Press, 1969.

Frame, Esther G. and Nathan T. Frame, *Reminiscences*. Cleveland: The Britton Printing Company, 1907.

Friends Ancient and Modern. no. 8. *Joseph Bevan Braithwaite*. New

York: David S. Taber, 1906.

Grubb, Edward. *Separations: Their Causes and Effects.* In *Studies in Nineteenth Century Quakerism.* London: Headley Brothers, 1914.

Henry, Marie. *The Secret Life of Hannah Whitall Smith.* Grand Rapids, Michigan: Chosen Books, 1984.

Jay, Allen. *Autobiography of Allen Jay.* Philadelphia: The John C. Winston Co., 1910.

Jay, Allen; Jay, Mahalah; and White, Thomas, N., ed. *Proceedings, including Declaration of Christian Doctrine, of the General Conference of Friends, held in Richmond, Ind., U.S.A., 1887.* Richmond, Indiana: Nicholson & Bro., 1887.

Johnson, Mary Coffin, ed. *Rhoda M. Coffin: Her Reminiscences, Addresses, Papers, and Ancestry.* New York: The Grafton Press, 1910.

Jones, Christina H. *American Friends in World Missions.* Elgin, Illinois: Brethren Publishing House, 1946.

Jones, Louis T. *The Quakers of Iowa.* Iowa City, Iowa: The State Historical Society of Iowa, 1914.

Jones, Rufus M. *The Later Periods of Quakerism.* 2 vols. London: MacMillan and Co., Ltd., 1921.

LeShana, David C. *Quakers in California: The Effects of 19th Century Revivalism on Western Quakerism.* Newberg, Oregon: The Barclay Press, 1969.

Mead, Edwin D. "Introduction." In *The Development of the Peace Idea and Other Essays.* ed. Sarah S. Trueblood. Norwood, Massachusettes: Plimptom Press, 1932.

Mekeel, Arthur J. *Quakerism and a Creed.* Philadelphia: Friends Book Store, 1936.

Moore, John M., ed. *Friends in the Delaware Valley: Philadelphia Yearly Meeting 1681-1981.* Haverford, Pennsylvania: Friends Historical Association, 1981.

Mott, Joanna Bowles. *Ephraim Bowles, His Quaker Heritage.* Des Moines, Iowa: J.J. Newlin, 1954.

Russell, Elbert. *The History of Quakerism.* Richmond, Indiana: Friends United Press, 1979.

Smith, Hannah Whitall. *John M. Whitall: The Story of His Life.* Philadelphia: Printed for the family, 1879.

Tebbetts, Charles E. *Biographical Sketch of the Late William Nicolson, M.D.* Richmond, Indiana: Nicholson Printing and Mfg. Co., 1909.

Thomas, Allen C. *The History of the Friends in America.*

Philadelphia: The John C. Winston Co., 1919.

Thomas, Anna Braithwaite. *J. Bevan Braithwaite: A Friend of the Nineteenth Century*. London: Hodder and Stoughton, 1909.

Thomas, Anna Braithwaite. *Life and Letters of Richard H. Thomas, M.D.* Philadelphia: The John C. Winston Company, 1905.

Trueblood, D. Elton. *The People called Quakers*. Richmond, Indiana: Friends United Press, 1980.

Votaw, A. H. "Allen Jay." In *Quaker Biographies*. sec. ii., v. 3, pp. 63-91. Philadelphia: For Sales at Friends' Book Store, 1920.

Williams, Walter R. *The Rich Heritage of Quakerism*. Grand Rapids, Michigan: William B. Eerdmans Publishing Company, 1962.

Wood, Richard E. "The Rise of Semi-Structured Worship and Paid Pastoral Leadership Among 'Gurneyite' Friends, 1850-1900." In *Quaker Worship in North America*. Edited by Francis B. Hall. Richmond, Indiana: Friends United Press, 1978.

Woodward, Walter C. *Timothy Nicholson: Master Quaker*. Richmond, Indiana: The Nicholson Press, 1927.

PERIODICALS

Allison, William J., ed. *Friends Review* 14 (Oct. 1860).

Friends' Intelligencer and Journal 44 (Oct. 1887).

The Friend (London) 27 (Nov. 1887).

Hartshorne, Henry, ed. *Friends' Review* 29 (Oct. 1875).

Hartshorne, Henry, ed. *Friends' Review* 40 (Jan. 1887).

Hartshorne, Henry, ed. *Friends' Review* 41 (Oct. 1887).

Hill, Daniel, ed. *The Christian Worker*. 12 (Sept. 1877).

Milne, George. "Letter to the Editor." *The British Friend* (May 1888).

Pollard, William. "Letter to the Editor." *The British Friend* (May 1888).

Pritchard, Calvin, ed. *The Christian Worker* 17 (Oct. 1887).

Rhoads, James E., ed. *Friends' Review* 32 (April 1879).

Scott, Richenda C. "Authority or Experience: John Wilhelm Rowntree and the Dilemma of 19th Century British Quakerism." *The Journal of the Friends' Historical Society* 49 (Spring 1960).

Trueblood, Benjamin F. "Creeds and Conferences." *The Christian Worker* 18 (March 1888).

Trueblood, Benjamin F. "Ministers' Wages." *The Christian Worker* 2 (Sept. 1872).

Trueblood, Benjamin F. "Ministers' Wages." *The Christian Worker* 2 (Oct. 1872).

Trueblood, Benjamin F. "The Twentieth Century Friend and His Bible School." *American Friend* 2 (July 1895).

Updegraff, David B. "The Light Within." *Friends' Review* 32 (April 1879).

Updegraff, David B., ed. *Friends' Expositor* 1 (July 1887).

Updegraff, David B., ed. *Friends' Expositor* 2 (April 1888).

Walton, Joseph, ed. *The Friend* 52 (April 1879).

Walton, Jospeh, ed. *The Friend* 60 (May 1887).

Walton, Joseph, ed. *The Friend* 61 (Oct. 1887).

Walton, Joseph, ed. *The Friend* 61 (Nov. 1887).

Westlake, Richard, ed. *The Friends' Quarterly Examiner* 86 (April 1888).

Whittier, John Greenleaf. "Letter to the Editor." *The Friend* 52 (May 1879).

MINUTES

Baltimore Yearly Meeting Minutes, 1870.
Baltimore Yearly Meeting Minutes, 1887.
Dublin Yearly Meeting Minutes, 1888.
Indiana Yearly Meeting Minutes, 1886.
Indiana Yearly Meeting Minutes, 1887.
Iowa Yearly Meeting Minutes, 1872.
Iowa Yearly Meeting Minutes, 1887.
Iowa Yearly Meeting Minutes, 1888.
Iowa Yearly Meeting Minutes, 1890.
Kansas Yearly Meeting Minutes, 1887.
London Yearly Meeting Minutes, 1871.
London Yearly Meeting Minutes, 1888.
New England Yearly Meeting Minutes, 1888.
New York Yearly Meeting Minutes, 1888.
North Carolina Yearly Meeting Minutes, 1888.
Ohio Yearly Meeting Minutes, 1879.
Ohio Yearly Meeting Minutes, 1888.
Western Yearly Meeting Minutes, 1870.
Western Yearly Meeting Minutes, 1875.
Western Yearly Meeting Minutes, 1888.

UNPUBLISHED RECORDS

Cox, Elizabeth Armstrong. "Memorial of John Henry Douglas." In Documents Dealing with the Life and Work of John Henry Douglas, Quaker Evangelist 1832-1919. Lilly Library Vault. Earlham College. Richmond, Indiana.

Fisher, B., Eugene. "A Study of Toleration among Midwest Quakers, 1850-1900." Master's thesis, Earlham School of Religion, 1972.

Furnas, Paul J. "Allen Jay: 1831-1910." Lecture delivered at 50th Anniversary of West Richmond Friends Meeting, Richmond, Indiana, 1959.

Hartshorne Family Papers. The Quaker Collection. Haverford College. Haverford, Pennsylvania.

Nicholson Papers. Lilly Library. Earlham College. Richmond, Indiana.

Redding, Earl W. "A Report to the General Board of Friends United Meeting Concerning the History of the Affirmation of Faith and Uniform Discipline in the Five Years Meeting of Friends." Oskaloosa, Iowa, 1974.

James Rhoads Papers. The Quaker Collection. Haverford College. Haverford, Pennsylvania.

Joseph Taylor Papers. The Quaker Collection. Haverford College. Haverford, Pennsylvania.